Focus on WRITING 2

www. myenglishlab.
com/writing

Helen Solórzano
David Wiese

John Beaumont, Series Editor
Borough of Manhattan Community College
City University of New York

ALWAYS LEARNING

PEARSON

Focus on Writing 2

Pearson Education, 10 Bank Street, White Plains, NY 10606

Staff Credits: The people who made up the *Focus on Writing 2* team, representing editorial, production, design, and manufacturing, are Pietro Alongi, Rhea Banker, Danielle Belfiore, Elizabeth Carlson, Nan Clarke, Aerin Csigay, Dave Dickey, Christine Edmonds, Oliva Fernandez, Barry Katzen, Penny Laporte, Jaime Lieber, Tara Maceyak, Amy McCormick, Barbara Perez, Joan Poole, Debbie Sistino, Jane Townsend, Paula Van Ells, and Adina Zoltan.

The Grammar Presentation charts in *Focus on Writing 2* are adapted from *Focus on Grammar 2, Fourth Edition*, by Irene E. Schoenberg, Pearson Education, White Plains, New York, © 2012.

Cover image: Shutterstock.com
Text composition: ElectraGraphics, Inc.
Text font: New Aster

Library of Congress Cataloging-in-Publication Data

Haugnes, Natasha, 1965–
 Focus on writing. 1 / Natasha Haugnes.
   p. cm.
 Includes index.
 ISBN 0-13-231350-2 — ISBN 0-13-231352-9 — ISBN 0-13-231353-7 — ISBN 0-13-231354-5 — ISBN 0-13-231355-3 1. English language—Textbooks for foreign speakers. 2. English language—Rhetoric—Problems, exercises, etc. 3. Report writing—Problems, exercises, etc. I. Title.
 PE1128.H3934 2011
 428.2—dc22

                                                                                2011014764

PEARSON LONGMAN ON THE **WEB**

Pearsonlongman.com offers online resources for teachers and students. Access our Companion Websites, our online catalog, and our local offices around the world.

Visit us at **pearsonlongman.com**.

Printed in the United States of America

ISBN 10: 0-13-231352-9
ISBN 13: 978-0-13-231352-0

15 2020

Contents

To the Teacher

Focus on Writing is a five-level series that prepares students for academic coursework. Each book in the series gives students an essential set of tools to ensure that they master not only the writing process, but also the grammatical structures, lexical knowledge, and rhetorical modes required for academic writing. The series provides an incremental course of instruction that progresses from basic sentences (Book 1) and paragraphs (Books 1–3) to essays (Books 3–5). Grammar presentation and focused grammar practice are correlated to *Focus on Grammar*.

A Process Approach to Writing

Over the past 30 years, the *writing process* approach has become the primary paradigm for teaching writing. As cognitive research shows, writing is a recursive process. When students practice the entire writing process repeatedly with careful guidance, they internalize the essential steps, thereby improving their writing and their confidence in themselves as writers.

Each unit in each book of *Focus on Writing* provides direct instruction, clear examples, and continual practice in the writing process. Students draw on their prior knowledge, set goals, gather information, organize ideas and evidence, and monitor their own writing process. Students write topic-related sentences and use them in a basic paragraph (Book 1); they focus on writing an *introduction*, *body*, and *conclusion* for a paragraph (Books 1–3) or essay (Books 3–5). Whether students are writing a group of related sentences, a paragraph, or an essay, they produce a complete, cohesive piece of writing in *every* unit.

Predictable Step-by-Step Units

Focus on Writing is easy to use. Its predictable and consistent unit format guides students step by step through the writing process.

▋ PLANNING FOR WRITING

Students are introduced to the unit theme through an engaging image and high-interest reading. Brainstorming tasks develop critical thinking and serve as a springboard for the unit's writing assignment. Vocabulary building activities and writing tips related to the topic and organizational focus of the unit provide opportunities for students to expand their own writing.

▋ STEP 1: PREWRITING

In Book 1, students learn the basics of sentence structure and are encouraged to combine sentences into cohesive paragraphs. They choose between two authentic academic writing assignments, explore their ideas through discussions with classmates, and complete a graphic organizer.

In Books 2–5, students learn the basics of a rhetorical structure (e.g., narration, description, opinion, persuasion, compare-contrast, cause-effect, or problem-solution) and choose between two authentic academic writing assignments. Students explore their ideas through freewriting, share them with classmates, and complete a graphic organizer.

STEP 2: WRITING THE FIRST DRAFT

Explanations, examples, and focused practice help students to prepare for their own writing assignment. Writing tasks guide students through the steps of the writing process as they analyze and develop topic sentences, body sentences, and concluding sentences (Books 1–3) and continue on to draft complete introductions, body paragraphs, and conclusions (Books 3–5). At all levels, students learn how to use transitions and other connecting words to knit the parts of their writing together.

STEP 3: REVISING

Before students revise their drafts, they read and analyze a writing model, complete vocabulary exercises, and review writing tips that they then apply to their own writing. A Revision Checklist tailored to the specific assignment guides students through the revision process.

STEP 4: EDITING

Grammar presentation and practice help students make the connection between grammar and writing. An Editing Checklist ensures students check and proofread their final drafts before giving them to their instructors.

Helpful Writing Tools

Each book in the series provides students with an array of writing tools to help them gain confidence in their writing skills.

- *Tip for Writers* presents a level-specific writing skill to help students with their assignment. The tips include asking *wh-* questions, using conjunctions to connect ideas, identifying audience, using descriptive details, and using pronoun referents.

- *Building Word Knowledge* sections give students explicit instruction in key vocabulary topics, for example, word families, collocations, compound nouns, and phrasal verbs.

- *Graphic organizers* help students generate and organize information for their writing assignment. For example, in Book 1, they fill out a timeline for a narrative paragraph and in Book 3, they complete a Venn diagram for a compare-contrast essay. In the final unit of Books 4 and 5, they use multiple organizers.

- *Sample paragraphs and essays* throughout the units, tied to the unit theme and writing assignments, provide clear models for students as they learn how to compose a topic sentence, thesis statement, introduction, body, and conclusion.

Carefully Targeted Grammar Instruction

Each unit in *Focus on Writing* helps students make the essential link between grammar and writing. The grammar topics for each unit are carefully chosen and correlated to *Focus on Grammar* to help students fulfill the writing goals of the unit.

Online Teacher's Manuals

The online Teacher's Manuals include model lesson plans, specific unit overviews, timed writing assignments, authentic student models for each assignment, rubrics targeted specifically for the writing assignment, and answer keys.

To the Student

Welcome to *Focus on Writing*! This book will help you develop your writing skills. You will learn about and practice the steps in the writing process.

All of the units are easy to follow. They include many examples, models and, of course, lots of writing activities.

Read the explanations on the next few pages before you begin Unit 1.

> Before you begin to write, you need to know what you will write about. A picture, a short reading, and a **brainstorming** activity will help you get ideas about a topic.

UNIT 5 Business Solutions

IN THIS UNIT You will write a paragraph about a business with a problem, and give possible solutions.

Some businesses just do not get it right. They do not accept credit cards. They close too early. Their prices are too high. Their stores are dirty or not organized well. They are not polite to customers. These businesses have problems. They need to find solutions or they will lose customers. What other kinds of problems can a business have?

Planning for Writing

■ BRAINSTORM

A. Read about Dina's business. What problem did it have? Was Dina's solution a good solution? Discuss your answer with a partner.

=== FASHION TO GO ===

Two years ago, Dina's dream came true. The 27-year-old fashion designer opened her own store. She finally had a place to sell her creative clothing, but there was one problem—she had no customers. Dina tried many ways to get customers. First, she made a new sign. Then, she advertised online and in the newspaper, but nothing worked. Finally, she discovered the problem. Her store was too far from downtown. People had to drive a long way to get to her store. In the end, Dina found an interesting solution to her problem. She closed the store and bought an old van. Now, she sells clothing from her van. She named her business "Fashion to Go." Each day, she drives to a different part of town. "I have customers all over the city," she laughs. Dina brought her clothes to her customers, and that is how she found success.

B. Using a Problem-Solution Chart. A problem-solution chart helps you think about problems and solutions. It helps you answer these questions: What is the problem? Why is it a problem? What are the solutions?

Read the article about Dina again. Work with a partner. Write the sentences in the problem-solution chart.

> She bought a van and sold her clothing in different places.
> She did not have any customers.
> The customers did not want to drive to the store.

Dina's Problem-Solution Chart

Problem
What was Dina's problem?
_____

Reasons
Why did Dina have the problem?
_____

Solutions
What was Dina's solution?
_____

103

A **reading** about the topic will help you develop more ideas. The reading can be a newspaper or magazine article, a webpage, or a blog.

Building Word Knowledge activities introduce a vocabulary or dictionary skill that you will be able to use when you write your assignment. For example, you will practice using different word forms and collocations.

■ READ

Read the article about Domino's Pizza.

Domino's Strange Advertising: Our Pizza Tastes Bad

1   In 2007, Domino's Pizza was in trouble. Customers were not happy. Profits[1] were down by 55 percent.

2   Domino's studied the negative comments people made about them on the Internet. Most people did not like Domino's pizza. "It's boring," said one customer. Others did not like the flavor. "The sauce is like ketchup," said one person. "It tastes like the pizza box," another person said.

3   How could Domino's solve its problems? They had three ideas:

(a) Pay a famous person to say the pizza tastes good.

(b) Ask the company president to travel across the country and say the pizza tastes good.

(c) Say the pizza tastes *bad*. Then promise to change it.

Surprisingly, Domino's chose option c.

4   In TV advertisements, Domino's employees[2] read the negative comments. They apologized for making bad pizza. Then they promised to make better pizza, with different cheese, different bread, and a new sauce.

5   The experts[3] did not think it was a good plan. They expected Domino's to lose more customers. But then something surprising happened. Sales went up immediately.

6   At first, Domino's thought customers were just curious about the new pizza flavor. They thought people would quickly lose interest. But sales stayed strong. By 2010, profits went up 55 percent.

7   What made Domino's "new pizza" a success? One expert explained, "Domino's said the product had problems, so the message was believable."

8   This was not the first promise that Domino's made to customers. In 1973, they promised to deliver[4] a pizza in 30 minutes. If not, the pizza was free. Domino's gave away a lot of pizzas, but they also got a lot of new customers. Soon, Domino's grew into an international company.

9   Today Domino's has over 9,000 stores in 60 countries. Clearly, other companies can learn from Domino's. In business, honesty is the most important ingredient.[5]

---

[1] **profit:** money that you gain by selling things or doing business, after you pay all other costs
[2] **employees:** people who are paid to work for someone else
[3] **expert:** someone who has special skill or knowledge of a subject
[4] **deliver:** to take food, packages, etc., to a particular place or person
[5] **ingredient:** a quality you need for success

Building Word Knowledge

Building Word Families. Many English words are part of a word family. When you learn a new word, it is helpful to learn other words in the same family. For example, many words have a related noun and verb form. Use a dictionary to help you find and use the correct word forms. Here are some examples.

Noun	Verb
expectation	*expect*
success	*succeed*
attraction	*attract*
increase	*increase*
improvement	*improve*

A. *Add the missing word forms. Use a dictionary to help you.*

Noun	Verb
1. _____	advertise
2. apology	_____
3. delivery	_____
4. explanation	_____
5. _____	promise
6. _____	sell
7. _____	suggest

B. *Complete the sentences. Write the correct word form.*

1. First Street Café does not _____ many customers.
   (attract / attraction)

2. The service at Lucky Garden Restaurant needs _____.
   (improve / improvement)

3. SuperShoes never gives an _____ for its mistakes.
   (apologize / apology)

4. The clothing store near my house is having a _____.
   (sale / sell)

5. Many restaurants _____ food to their customers.
   (deliver / delivery)

6. The customer service people can _____ the problem.
   (explain / explanation)

7. I have many good _____ for the company.
   (suggest / suggestions)

■ STEP 1: PREWRITING

This section helps you further develop your ideas. It gives you a short explanation of the writing assignment.

The **Your Own Writing** section gives you a choice of two writing assignments. After you choose one of the assignments, you can begin to think about what you will write and share your ideas with a partner (**Checking In**). Putting your ideas into a **graphic organizer** will help you structure your ideas.

Writing a Problem-Solution Paragraph

In this unit, you are going to write a problem-solution paragraph. Like other paragraphs, the topic sentence of a problem-solution paragraph says the topic and controlling idea. The body of a problem-solution paragraph has two parts: The first part explains the problem, and the second part suggests a solution to the problem. The concluding sentence often restates the idea in the topic sentence or gives a final thought. The final thought is often a prediction, or guess about the future.

> **The Problem-Solution Paragraph**
> ▶ Topic Sentence
> ▶ Body Sentences
> ▶ Concluding Sentence

Step 1   Prewriting

Prewriting helps you think about ideas for your assignment. In this prewriting, you choose your assignment, and you write and discuss ideas about the problem and solution. Then you make a problem-solution chart to organize ideas for your writing.

Your Own Writing

Choosing Your Assignment

A. *Choose Assignment 1 or Assignment 2.*

Assignment 1: Write about a large business—a company or corporation—with a problem. Describe the problem. Then suggest solutions.

Assignment 2: Write about a small, local business with a problem. A local business is a business in your neighborhood or town. Describe the problem. Then suggest solutions.

B. *Make a list of companies or local businesses. Use the ideas below or your own ideas. Check (✓) the companies or businesses with problems. Then choose a company or business for your assignment.*

Companies and Corporations	**Local Businesses**
Restaurant chain: _____*Domino's*_____	Local restaurant: _____
Automobile company: _____	Clothing store: _____*Fashion to Go*_____
Computer company: _____	Bookstore: _____
Food company: _____	Grocery store: _____
Your own idea: _____	Your own idea: _____

C. *Freewrite for five minutes about your assignment topic. Write all ideas. Keep writing. Do not worry about good or bad ideas. Write any ideas you have about the topic. Here are some questions to get you started.*

• What do you know about this business?

• Why does this business interest you?   ➡

• What problems does the business have?

• Why does it have these problems?

• What solutions can you suggest?

D. Checking In. *Share your ideas with a partner. Ask your partner questions and find out about the problem. For example:*

• What is the company or business?

• What is the problem?

• What are some reasons for the problem?

Share your own opinions about the problem. Is it an interesting problem? Are there good solutions? Do you need more information?

After your discussion, add new ideas to your freewriting, if helpful.

E. *Complete the problem-solution chart for your assignment. Write the name of the company or business. Write the problems, the reasons for the problems, and possible solutions.*

Company or Business Name: _____

Problem
_____

⬇

Reasons
_____
_____
_____

⬇

Solutions
_____
_____
_____

STEP 2: WRITING THE FIRST DRAFT

This section guides you through each part of your writing assignment. For a paragraph assignment, you will learn how to write a topic sentence, body sentences, and a concluding sentence. At the end of Step 2, you will be able to write a complete first draft.

> **Focused Practice** activities will give you lots of writing practice *before* you draft your writing assignment. Make sure to look at all of the examples and models before you complete the exercises. A useful **Tip for Writers** gives you specific writing tools, for example, guidelines for correct punctuation.

Step 2   Writing the First Draft

THE TOPIC SENTENCE

The topic sentence of a paragraph includes the topic and controlling idea of the paragraph. In the problem-solution paragraph for this unit, the topic is the name of the company or business. The controlling idea is the problem. The topic sentence can also give background information about the topic. The background information answers questions such as:

- Where is the business?
- What is the business?

The Problem-Solution Paragraph

▼ Topic Sentence
  · Topic and Controlling Idea
  · Background Information
▶ Body Sentences
▶ Concluding Sentence

Example:

　　　topic　　　　　　background information　　　controlling idea
Lucky Garden restaurant, a Chinese restaurant near my house, is always empty.

controlling idea　　topic　　　　background information
No one eats at Lucky Garden, a Chinese restaurant near my house.

Tip for Writers

Punctuation. Background information is extra information. It helps the reader understand the topic better. Use commas to separate the background information in your topic sentence. The commas show which words are part of the topic and controlling idea, and which words are part of the background information. Here are some examples.

*The Royal Theater, **a movie theater in my town,** is not popular.*

*Nobody likes to see movies at The Royal Theater, **a movie theater in my town.***

Note: When the background information follows the subject, use a comma before and after the background information. When the background information is at the end of the sentence, put a comma in front of the background information.

Underline the background information. Add commas.

1. Fishermen's Bounty a local seafood store is not a good place to buy fish.
2. It is difficult to get a table at Fresh a new restaurant downtown.
3. WorldwideTransport an international delivery service is not dependable.
4. MultiStar Energy a power company hurts the environment.
5. People do not buy computers from Comp Buy a large computer company.
6. Best Shoes In Town a new shoe store in my neighborhood is not very successful.

Business Solutions **109**

Focused Practice

A. *Read the topic sentences. Circle the topic. Underline the controlling idea. Double underline the background information.*

Example:

(MXL Motors,) an American car company, only makes luxury cars.

1. Pat's Corner, a small bookstore in my neighborhood, has very few customers.
2. Easy Auto, a local car repair shop, is not convenient.
3. A lot of young people do not like Perfect Fits, a clothing store.
4. George's Diner, the restaurant next door to our school, is usually empty.
5. No one buys computers from TechTown, a computer store downtown.

B. *Look at Exercise A. Which questions does the background information answer? Check (✓) the questions.*

	Where is the business?	What is the business?
1. Pat's Corner	✓	✓
2. Easy Auto		
3. Perfect Fits		
4. George's Diner		
5. TechTown		

C. *Read the paragraphs. Circle and write the best topic sentence for each paragraph. Discuss your answers with a partner.*

Paragraph 1

> **News for Today**
>
> _____
>
> The first problem is the website. Most people read news online, but the *News for Today* website is not well designed. It is difficult to read. Some sections of the newspaper are hard to find online. Another problem is that the paper does not have enough reporters to report all the local news, so people look for news on TV or in other newspapers. To solve this problem, *News for Today* should improve the website and hire more reporters. In this way, it will attract more readers.

110   UNIT 5

■ STEP 3: REVISING

After you write your first draft, you aren't finished yet! Step 3 shows you how to revise your draft to make your writing better. Revising means changing sentences or words or ideas. When you revise, you try to make your writing clearer for the reader.

> Review and analyze the **model** paragraphs to get an idea of what a well-written paragraph looks like. You may see another Tip for Writers or Building Word Knowledge box to help you fit the parts of your own writing together.
>
> Completing the **Revision Checklists** for each writing assignment will help you identify parts of your draft that need improvement.

Step 3   Revising

Revising your work is an important part of the writing process. You can make sure that your paragraph has enough information and that the information supports the topic sentence.

Focused Practice

A. *Read the persuasive paragraph.*

Posting Class Assignments Online

I think that posting class assignments online is a good idea. First of all, students can check the dates of important exams and assignments easily. For instance, my math teacher has a web page. She uploads her class schedule there. We can check the date of our math exams on her web page. In addition, teachers can save paper. For example, my history teacher uses a lot of paper to print homework instructions. It is not necessary. He can post the homework instructions online and save hundreds of pieces of paper. Clearly, teachers should post their class assignments online.

B. *Work with a partner. Answer the questions about the paragraph.*

1. What is the topic of the paragraph? Circle it.
2. What is the controlling idea of the paragraph (the writer's opinion)? Underline it.
3. What reasons support the writer's opinion? Put a star (*) next to the reasons.
4. What examples explain the reasons? Put a check (✓) next to the examples.
5. What is the concluding sentence? Underline it.

Your Own Writing

Revising Your Draft

A. *Reread the first draft of your paragraph. Use the Revision Checklist. What do you need to revise?*
B. *Revise your paragraph.*

Revision Checklist

Did you . . .
- ☐ give an opinion about sharing information on the Internet?
- ☐ give reasons and examples for your opinion?
- ☐ restate your opinion and give advice in the concluding sentence?

STEP 4: EDITING

In the final step, you review a grammar topic that will help you edit your revised draft. Then you use an Editing Checklist to correct your own paragraph for any errors in grammar, punctuation, or capitalization.

Grammar Presentation charts present notes and examples on specific grammar topics related to your writing assignment. Follow up with grammar practice.

Editing Checklists for each writing assignment help you correct and polish your final draft.

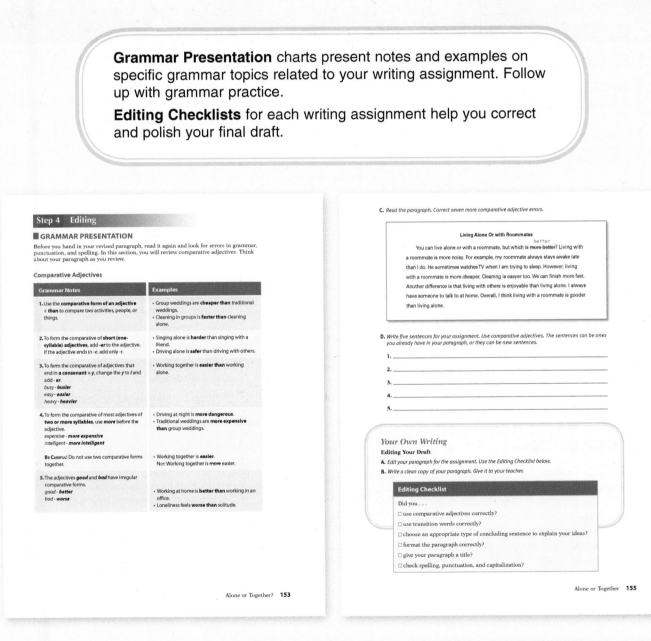

Now, you are ready to begin with Unit 1. Enjoy the writing process!

Scope and Sequence

UNIT	STEP 1 Planning and Prewriting	STEP 2 Writing the First Draft
1 Celebrations *Writing Focus* Writing a basic paragraph *Reading* *April Fool's Day,* about celebrating April Fool's Day	Using a *wh-* questions chart Using prepositions for time and place Using words for celebrations Thinking about audience Choosing a writing assignment for a paragraph about a holiday or special event Freewriting about the topic Sharing ideas and creating a *wh-* questions chart	Writing the topic sentence, controlling idea, body sentences, and concluding sentence Supporting the topic sentence Finding information online about a holiday or special event Using collocations Using capital letters Writing paragraph titles Writing a paragraph about celebrations
2 Everyday Heroes *Writing Focus* Writing an opinion paragraph *Reading* *Principal for a Day,* about a young girl who becomes the principal of her school	Using a descriptive wheel Using verbs to describe admiration Connecting ideas with *because* Choosing a writing assignment for an opinion paragraph Freewriting about the topic Sharing ideas and creating a descriptive wheel	Writing a topic sentence and controlling idea for an opinion paragraph Finding information online about admirable people Using examples in body sentences Writing a concluding sentence that restates the topic sentence Using synonyms Writing an opinion paragraph about an admirable person
3 Turning Points *Writing Focus* Writing a narrative paragraph *Reading* *Across the Street, a Long-Lost Brother,* about a turning point in someone's life	Using a timeline Using collocations Joining ideas with *and, but,* and *so* Choosing a writing assignment for a narrative paragraph Freewriting about the topic Sharing ideas and creating a timeline	Writing a topic sentence and controlling idea for a narrative paragraph Finding information online about a turning point or memorable event Using time order and background information Writing a concluding sentence that restates the topic sentence and adds a final thought Using concluding connectors Writing a narrative paragraph about a memorable event

STEP 3 Revising	STEP 4 Editing	Learning Outcome	*Focus on Grammar Level 2, Fourth Edition*
Formatting a paragraph Analyzing a model paragraph Applying the Revision Checklist and writing the second draft	Reviewing simple present statements Incorporating the grammar in sentences Applying the Editing Checklist and writing the final draft	Can write very short, basic descriptions of special events and celebrations	**Unit 8** Simple Present: Affirmative and Negative Statements
Using clauses with *because* Analyzing a model paragraph Applying the Revision Checklist and writing the second draft	Reviewing descriptive adjectives Incorporating the grammar in sentences Applying the Editing Checklist and writing the final draft	Can write a short, clear paragraph that supports and gives reasons for an opinion Can describe, in simple terms, family and people in his/her environment	**Unit 5** Descriptive Adjectives
Analyzing a model paragraph Applying the Revision Checklist and writing the second draft	Reviewing the simple past of regular and irregular verbs Incorporating the grammar in sentences Applying the Editing Checklist and writing the final draft	Can connect sentences in a short paragraph to tell a story	**Unit 18** Simple Past: Affirmative and Negative Statements with Regular Verbs **Unit 19** Simple Past: Affirmative and Negative Statements with Irregular Verbs

UNIT	STEP 1 Planning and Prewriting	STEP 2 Writing the First Draft
4 Too Much Information *Writing Focus* Writing a persuasive paragraph *Reading* *Don't Just Surf the Web–Be the Web,* about putting yourself online	Using a T-chart Recognizing Internet vocabulary Thinking about audience Choosing a writing assignment for a persuasive paragraph Freewriting about the topic Sharing ideas and creating a T-chart	Writing a topic sentence and controlling idea for a persuasive paragraph Identifying facts and opinions Finding information online about websites Using reasons, details, facts and examples in body sentences Using transition words to introduce reasons Writing a concluding sentence that gives advice Writing a persuasive paragraph about having an online presence
5 Business Solutions *Writing Focus* Writing a problem-solution paragraph *Reading* *Domino's Strange Advertising: Our Pizza Tastes Bad,* about Domino's successful advertising strategy	Using a problem-solution chart Using word families Choosing a writing assignment for a problem-solution paragraph Freewriting about the topic Sharing ideas and creating a problem-solution chart	Writing the topic sentence and controlling idea for a problem-solution paragraph Including background information Writing about cause and effect Using descriptive adjectives Finding information online about business problems Making a prediction and referring to solutions in concluding sentences Writing a paragraph about a business problem and solutions
6 Alone or Together? *Writing Focus* Writing a compare-contrast paragraph *Reading* *Together Is Better Than Alone,* about new types of group activities	Using a Venn diagram Using compound nouns Choosing a writing assignment for a compare-contrast paragraph Freewriting about the topic Sharing ideas and creating a Venn diagram	Writing the topic sentence, controlling idea, body sentences, and concluding sentence for a compare-contrast paragraph Using gerunds Explaining similarities and differences Using words for similarity and difference Finding information online about activities Writing a paragraph about activities

STEP 3 Revising	STEP 4 Editing	Learning Outcome	*Focus on Grammar Level 2, Fourth Edition*
Analyzing a model paragraph Applying the Revision Checklist and writing the second draft	Reviewing modal verbs Incorporating the grammar in sentences Applying the Editing Checklist and writing the final draft	Can write a short, clear paragraph that supports and gives reasons for an opinion Can describe something in a simple list of points	**Unit 13** Ability: *Can / Could* **Unit 25** *Will* for the Future **Unit 26** *May* or *Might* for Possibility **Unit 30** Advice: Should, Ought to, Had better
Analyzing a model paragraph Applying the Revision Checklist and writing the second draft	Reviewing count and non-count nouns Incorporating the grammar in sentences Applying the Editing Checklist and writing the final draft	Can explain the main points of an idea or problem in a short, simple paragraph	**Unit 4** Count Nouns and Proper Nouns **Unit 27** Count and Non-Count Nouns, Quantifiers, Articles
Using sentence variety Analyzing a model paragraph Applying the Revision Checklist and writing the second draft	Reviewing comparative adjectives Incorporating the grammar in sentences Applying the Editing Checklist and writing the final draft	Can describe, in simple terms, aspects of his/her background and immediate environment Can give a simple description of likes and dislikes	**Unit 33** The Comparative

Celebrations

IN THIS UNIT   You will write a paragraph about a holiday or special event.

All over the world, people celebrate holidays and special events. Some people celebrate events in history, important people, or religious beliefs. Some people celebrate special events, such as marriages, anniversaries, and graduations. On these holidays and special event days, people spend time with family and friends. They often eat special food, listen to special music, or wear special clothing. What holidays and special events do you celebrate? How do you celebrate them?

Planning for Writing

■ BRAINSTORM

A. *Read the invitations. What similar events do you celebrate? Discuss your answers with a partner.*

1.

You're invited!
Celebrate Ross & Nancy's
5th Anniversary.
Time: 8:00 P.M. on Saturday, June 25
Place: Ricardo's Restaurant on First Street

2.

Julia's first birthday!
Come to the party at Grandma Rose's house.
Sunday, August 2 at 2:00 o'clock
We'll serve cake and ice cream.
You bring a dish to share.

3.

New Year's Eve
Black & White Ball
Dance all night!
On December 31 at the Majestic Hotel
Dinner at 8:00 P.M.
Dancing begins at 10:00 P.M.
Please wear black and white.

4.

He was born in 1935.
He became "The King of Rock and Roll."
Join us for the
Elvis Presley Birthday Celebration
on Sunday at Graceland.
Check our website for details.

B. Using a *Wh-* Questions Chart. A *wh-* questions chart helps you think of ideas for your writing. Answer the *wh-* questions **who**, **what**, **where**, **when**, and **why** about events. It will help you think of details and describe the events.

Look at the wh- *questions chart. Complete the left column with information from invitation 2. Then work with a partner. Choose another invitation and complete the right column.*

	Invitation #2	**Invitation # _____**
Who?	Julia	
What?		
Where?	Grandma Rose's house	
When?		
Why?	birthday	

Read the online article about April Fool's Day.

April Fool's Day

1 April Fool's Day is a strange holiday. It is not a vacation day. It is not a religious holiday. There are no special clothes, meals, or songs for this day. It is just a day for fooling[1] people. Every year on April 1, it becomes OK to play tricks on people—to make them believe things that are not true.

2 Here are some tricks people sometimes play on April Fool's Day.

> Trick #1: Change the time on someone's alarm clock.

> Trick #2: Call someone and leave a funny phone message. Say: *"Ella Phant"* or *"Anna Mal" called. Please call her back today at home.* Then give the phone number for the zoo.

> Trick #3: On a busy street, glue[2] money to the sidewalk. Then watch people try to pick it up!

3 On April Fool's Day, you try to make other people believe your trick. Then they can have a good laugh when they discover it is not really true, but be careful. Your friends and family may try to fool you too. Even newspapers and TV shows may join the fun. For example, in 1957, a British news show reported about a "spaghetti farm"[3] on TV. It said spaghetti grew on special trees in Italy. Many people believed the story. Some even called the show and asked, "How can I grow a spaghetti tree?"

4 Few people are safe from April Fool's tricks. It is a worldwide event. People celebrate the holiday in the United States, France, Italy, Brazil, Japan, China, and many other countries.

5 The holiday is very popular, but we do not know where it comes from. Some people say it is from England. Others say it is from France because in the late 1500s, France changed the date of New Year's from April 1 to January 1. When people forgot the new date, they were called an "April fool." The tradition may also come from the Middle East. In Iran, people sometimes play tricks during Sizdah Be-dar, a holiday on April 1 or 2.

6 When you plan your tricks for the next April Fool's Day, remember a few things. First, in some countries, such as England, Australia, and South Africa, the tricks have to stop at 12:00 noon. Also, make sure your tricks are safe. No one should get hurt. Finally, remember that if you fool people, they may try to fool you later. Other than that, have fun!

---

[1] **fooling:** making someone believe something that is not true
[2] **glue:** to use a sticky substance to join things together
[3] **farm:** an area of land for raising food

Building Word Knowledge

Prepositions for Time and Place. When you write about a holiday or special event, it is helpful to include the date, the time, and the place of the event. Use the prepositions *in*, *on*, and *at* plus a date, time, or place in your writing about holidays and events. Here are some examples.

in + year / month	*Elvis was born* **in 1935**.
on + date	*Come and dance all night* **on December 31**.
at + time	*Dinner is* **at 8:00 P.M.**
in + country / city	*The Graceland Mansion is* **in Memphis**.
on + street	*Ricardo's Restaurant is* **on First Street**.
at + address / place	*Come to the party* **at Grandma Rose's house**.

Complete the sentences. Use **in, on,** *or* **at.**

1. _____ 1957, a British news show reported that spaghetti grew on trees.

2. _____ a busy street, glue money to a sidewalk.

3. _____ Iran, people sometimes play tricks during Sizdah Be-dar.

4. April Fool's Day takes place _____ April 1.

5. The tricks have to stop _____ 12:00 noon.

Focused Practice

A. *Read the article again. Are these sentences True (T) or False (F)? Write* T *or* F.

_____ **1.** On April Fool's Day, people play tricks on each other.

_____ **2.** According to the reading, people get angry when they find out that something is not true.

_____ **3.** In 1957, a newspaper in Italy said that spaghetti grew on special spaghetti trees.

_____ **4.** April Fool's Day is only celebrated in the United States.

_____ **5.** We know how the April Fool's Day holiday began.

_____ **6.** Everyone celebrates April Fool's Day the same way.

B. *Work with a partner. Make a list of the things you can and cannot do on April Fool's Day.*

You can . . .	You cannot . . .
play tricks on people	

C. *Make inferences (good guesses) about April Fool's Day around the world. Read the sentences and check (✓) Agree or Disagree. Discuss your answers with a partner.*

	Agree	**Disagree**
1. Most people enjoy playing tricks on each other.	☐	☐
2. Children enjoy April Fool's Day more than adults.	☐	☐
3. Businesses, government offices, and schools usually close on April Fool's Day.	☐	☐

D. *Think about the reading. Discuss your answers with a partner.*

1. Do you celebrate April Fool's Day? Do you want to? Why or why not?

2. Do you think it is funny to play tricks on people? Do you want people to play tricks on you? Why or why not?

3. Can you think of any other funny or unusual holidays? What do people do on those holidays?

Tip for Writers

Audience. It is important for a writer to think about audience. The audience is the person who will read your writing. Remember, you know a lot about your topic, but your readers may not know anything about it. Make sure you include the information your readers need to understand your ideas. Here is an example.

We celebrate Old Home Day.

You probably have these questions about this sentence.

- What is "Old Home Day"?
- Who is "we"?
- Why do people celebrate it?

As you write, think about your readers. Ask yourself questions to answer for your readers.

Read the sentences. Which questions do the sentences answer? Check (✓) them. Which questions are not answered for the reader? Put an X next to them.

1. We celebrate Jamhuri Day every year.

_____ Who is "we"?

_____ When do we celebrate Jamhuri Day?

2. Nana's birthday is a special event.

_____ Who is "Nana"?

_____ What is the special event?

3. May Day is an international celebration.

_____ Why do people celebrate May Day?

_____ Where do people celebrate it?

4. Everyone celebrates Children's Day.

_____ Who celebrates Children's Day?

_____ Why do people celebrate it?

Writing a Paragraph

In this unit, you are going to write a paragraph about a holiday or special event. A paragraph is a group of sentences about one idea. A paragraph includes a topic sentence, body sentences, and a concluding sentence.

> **The Basic Paragraph**
>
> ▶ Topic Sentence
> ▶ Body Sentences
> ▶ Concluding Sentence

- The topic sentence gives the controlling idea of the paragraph. It is often the first sentence in the paragraph.

- The body sentences support the controlling idea. They give specific facts and details to explain the controlling idea.

- The concluding sentence often repeats the idea in the topic sentence. It is usually the last sentence in the paragraph.

Step 1   Prewriting

Prewriting is an important step in the writing process. It helps you choose your topic and get ideas for your paragraph. In this prewriting, first you choose your assignment. Then you begin to think of ideas for the assignment.

Your Own Writing

Choosing Your Assignment

A. *Choose Assignment 1 or Assignment 2.*

Assignment 1: Write about a holiday that many people celebrate.

Assignment 2: Write about a special event that you celebrate with family and friends.

B. *Look at the list of holidays and special events. Check (✔) the ones you celebrate and add your own ideas. Then choose a holiday or special event to write about.*

Holidays	**Special Events**
_____ New Year's Eve	_____ Wedding anniversary
_____ National holidays	_____ Birthday
_____ Religious holidays	_____ Graduation

Your own ideas:

_____

_____

_____

Your own ideas:

_____

_____

_____

C. Freewriting is a way to get ideas for your writing. When you freewrite, you write about your topic for a few minutes without stopping. You do not think about whether your ideas are good or bad. You do not worry about grammar or spelling. You just write down your ideas. Later, you can choose ideas from your freewriting for your paragraph.

Freewrite for 5 minutes about your holiday or special event. Here are some questions to get you started:

- What is the name of the holiday or event?

- How do you celebrate it?

- Who celebrates it?

- Is there any special food, music, or clothing for the event?

D. Checking in. *Share your ideas with a partner. Ask your partner questions and find out about your partner's event or holiday. For example:*

- When does it take place?

- Where does it take place?

- Why do people celebrate it?

After your discussion, add new ideas to your freewriting.

E. *Complete the* wh- *questions chart for your assignment. Write the name of your holiday or event. Then answer the questions.*

Holiday or Event:
Who?
What?
Where?
When?
Why?

Building Word Knowledge

Words for Celebrations. There are many types of holidays and special events, and different ways of celebrating them. English has several names for these events and celebrations. Here are some examples.

a festival	a time of public celebration *Everyone in town comes to the winter* **festival**.
a ceremony	a formal or traditional set of actions used at an important social or religious event *The couple got married in a religious* **ceremony**.
a party	a gathering when people enjoy themselves by eating, drinking, dancing *We had a* **party** *to celebrate our graduation.*
a parade	a walk or march together to celebrate something *Thousands of people come to watch the Chinese New Year* **parade**.
a reunion	a meeting of friends, family members, or classmates after a long time away from each other *I saw all my old classmates at my high school* **reunion**.

Complete the sentences. Use the words for celebrations.

1. Last weekend, my friends came to my house for a _____. We talked, listened to music, and danced.

2. My family is really big, with a lot of aunts, uncles, and cousins. We all live far apart, but every two years, we meet in one place for a family _____.

3. On Independence Day, there is a big _____ through town. A long line of people walk in the main street, including soldiers in uniform and people playing music.

4. At the end of high school, we had a graduation _____. The principal and students made speeches, and then the students got their diplomas.

5. My town has a summer _____ in June. People come to my town and we sing songs, dance, and play games.

■ THE TOPIC SENTENCE

The topic sentence is usually the first sentence in a paragraph. It includes the topic of the paragraph and a controlling idea. The topic answers the question *What is the paragraph about?* The controlling idea answers the question *What does the paragraph explain about the topic?* For this assignment, the topic sentence can answer these questions:

The Basic Paragraph

▼ Topic Sentence
  • Topic
  • Controlling Idea

▶ Body Sentences
▶ Concluding Sentence

- What is the holiday or special event?
- Who celebrates it?
- Why do people celebrate it?

Example:

Teachers Day in Colombia

Teachers Day is the day when students and parents thank teachers for their hard work. It takes place every May 15 in Colombia. All around the country, students prepare songs, dances, and poems for their teachers. The students give their teachers thank-you cards and small gifts. At some schools, teachers have a special lunch together. Some schools also give teachers awards for their work. Teachers help students a lot, so it is important to have a day to thank teachers.

The **topic sentence** is: *Teachers Day is the day when students and parents thank teachers for their hard work.*

The **topic** is: *Teachers Day.* All the sentences in the paragraph are about Teachers Day.

The **controlling idea** is: *the day when students and parents thank teachers for their hard work.* All the sentences explain how people thank teachers for their hard work.

Focused Practice

A. *Circle the topic of each sentence. Underline the controlling idea.*

Example:

(Teachers Day) is a day to thank teachers for their hard work.

1. Community Service Day is a day to help other people in our community.

2. Chuseok is a traditional holiday in Korea. all relatives gather to celebrate erey year in Sept.

3. New Year's Eve is a fun event in New York City.

4. The Running of the Bulls (San Fermín) is an exciting event in Pamplona, Spain.

5. Jamhuri Day is a patriotic holiday in Kenya.

6. new Year's Eve is a big celebration in Brazil.

B. *Read the pairs of sentences. Check (✓) the best topic sentence in each pair for the assignment in this unit.*

Example:

___✓___ **a.** The Fourth of July is a patriotic holiday in the United States.

_____ **b.** There are fireworks and concerts on the Fourth of July.

1. __✓__ **a.** My whole family celebrates my grandmother Nana's birthday.

   _____ **b.** My grandmother Nana is a kind and loving person.

2. _____ **a.** Chocolate and flowers are traditional Valentine's Day gifts.

   __✓__ **b.** Valentine's Day is a celebration of love and friendship.

3. _____ **a.** Nelson Mandela was a great man.

   __✓__ **b.** Mandela Day celebrates the life and work of Nelson Mandela.

4. __✓__ **a.** My roommates and I have movie night every Friday.

   _____ **b.** My roommates and I like to watch movies.

C. *Read the paragraphs. Choose the best topic sentence for each paragraph. Write it on the lines.*

Paragraph 1

Celebrating a Special Event

_____

_____

In 1915, my great grandfather, John Brown, married Ida Mae Williams, and they had seven children. Today, members of the Brown family live all over the world. In the first week of July, family members come to Atlanta, Georgia, for a big family party. We learn about the history of the Brown family. We watch a slide show about John, Ida Mae, and their children. We meet all our aunts, uncles, and cousins. The children play games and go swimming. At night, we have a barbeque. We cook chicken and eat traditional food such as corn bread and beans. Some family members bring musical instruments, and we play music and sing. Our family reunion is fun and makes me proud to be part of the Brown family.

---

   a. My family is close and we enjoy spending time together.

   b. A family reunion is a time for families to get together.

✗ **c.** Every year my family goes to the Brown Family Reunion.

Paragraph 2

Sunday

_____

_____

My family works very hard during the week, but on Sunday we just have fun. My father does not go to work at his factory. My mother does not cook or clean. My sister and I do not study. We just relax and spend time together as a family. In the morning, we get up late. Then we go to the park, and we play games together. On rainy days, we go to the movies. We always go to a restaurant for dinner. I want every day to be like Sunday.

    a. On Sundays, my family watches movies.

✗ **b.** Sunday is a day of rest for my family.

    c. Everyone likes Sundays.

Your Own Writing

chuseok (Korea)

Finding Out More

A. *Go online. Type the keyword* [the name of your holiday or special event]. *Find information about your holiday or special event. Look for new ideas and new words for your paragraph.*

B. *Answer the questions.*

  1. What is the name of the holiday or event? _Thanksgiving_

  2. Who celebrates this holiday or event? _People all over The USA_

  3. Why do people celebrate it? _People celebrate it in memoria_

  4. Other information: _Colonist s Plymonth and native america people, shared food and harvest and other ble ssing of The past year. Its start in 1621._

C. *Checking in. Share your information with a partner. Did your partner . . .*

  • find interesting information about the holiday or special event?

  • write information to help you understand the event?

  • include any ideas you can use in your writing?

After your discussion, add new ideas to your information, if helpful.

➡

grateful

Planning Your Topic Sentence

Thanksgiven is time For us to remember to be grateful cause the families celebrated together and the family stay together.

A. Write two topic sentences for your paragraph. Use your wh-questions chart on page 8, and your information in Finding Out More to help you.

Thanksgive is a holiday in USA. Celebrated on the fouth Thurday of november.

B. Read your sentences. Circle the ⬚topic⬚ and underline the controlling idea in each sentence. Then choose the best topic sentence for your paragraph.

■ THE BODY SENTENCES

The body sentences in a paragraph develop and support the controlling idea in the topic sentence. They give information and details to explain the topic and controlling idea. The body sentences should not have information about other topics.

The Basic Paragraph

▶ Topic Sentence

▼ Body Sentences

　• Development and Support

▶ Concluding Sentence

Example:

New Year's Eve

New Year's Eve is a fun event in New York City. The event takes place at night on December 31 each year. Thousands of people come to Times Square in New York City, and millions of people watch the celebration on TV. The square is closed to traffic. Everyone stands in the middle of the square. There is a big stage, and famous singers perform for the crowd. At midnight, a giant ball of lights falls from the top of a building. People cheer and sing a traditional song, "Auld Lang Syne." Everyone in Times Square is happy and has a good time on New Year's Eve.

The **topic** is: *New Year's Eve in New York City*

The **controlling idea** is: *It is a fun event.*

These **details** are in the body sentences. They support the topic sentence and the controlling idea. They explain *what* happens during the event and *why* the event is fun.

- *Thousands of people come to Times Square.*
- *Millions of people watch the celebration on TV.*
- *Famous singers perform.*

(continued)

- *At midnight, a giant ball of lights falls from the top of a building.*
- *People cheer and sing.*

These details are *not* in the body sentences. They do *not* support the topic sentence and the controlling idea.

- *Sometimes people get very cold and have to go to the hospital.* (This sentence does not support the idea that the event is fun).
- *I want to go to New York for New Year's Eve next year.* (This sentence is about the writer, not the holiday.)
- *There are big New Year's Eve celebrations in other cities around the world.* (This sentence is about cities in other countries, not New York.)
- *There is a big parade in New York on Thanksgiving Day.* (This sentence is about another holiday.)

Focused Practice

A. Underline the topic sentence in each paragraph. Circle the controlling idea. Then read the paragraphs. Cross out the two sentences in each paragraph that do not support the topic sentence.

Paragraph 1

Melbourne Cup Day

Everything stops in Melbourne, Australia, for Melbourne Cup Day, a day everyone enjoys. The Melbourne Cup is a famous horse race. It takes place on the first Tuesday in November. At 3 P.M. in the city of Melbourne, schools and businesses close. The streets are empty. Everyone watches the races. We also have a famous boat race and swimming competition, called The Royal Hobart Regatta. People all over Australia come and cheer for their favorite horses. Last year, my favorite horse won. About 120,000 people go to the race. People dress up for this special day. Men wear new suits, and women wear fancy dresses and hats. Melbourne Cup Day is fun for all Australians.

[Handwritten annotations: "TS" appears twice, "opnion" written beside "Last year, my favorite horse won", and "Opnion is not good" written below the box.]

Paragraph 2

HW

Community Service Day

(Community Service Day) is a day to help other people in our community. It happens every year at my school. On Community Service Day, the students do volunteer work to help other people. We also have a party to celebrate graduation *N B* at the end of the year. The week before Community Service Day, the students sign up to work at different places. For example, people serve food at a homeless shelter, paint the walls of a school, or clean a park. On the morning of Community Service Day, we meet at school. School buses drive us to our jobs for the day. We spend all day working. Some of the jobs are really boring. *not B* After we return to school, we have a pizza party. We are all very tired, but we feel good because we helped other people.) *not put your opnion*

B. *Work with a partner. Compare your crossed out sentences in Exercise A. Why do they not support the topic sentence?*

C. *Read the topic sentence. Circle the topic and underline the controlling idea. Check (✓) the seven body sentences that best support the controlling idea.*

1 **Topic Sentence:** (Jamhuri Day) is a patriotic holiday in Kenya.

2G ___✓__ It takes place every December 12.

3G ___✓__ On this day in 1963, Kenya became an independent country.

___✗__ In the United States, people celebrate Independence Day on July 4.

___✗__ In Kenya, we also celebrate Kenyatta Day on October 20.

Conclusion 8 G ___✓__ Kenyans have many ways to celebrate their freedom.

___✗__ I'm very proud to be Kenyan.

4 G ___✓__ People watch parades and play games in parks.

5 G ___✓__ They perform traditional music and dances.

___✗__ I am learning to do some traditional dances.

6 ___✓__ Many Kenyans also wear traditional clothing on this day.

___✗__ On most days, people do not wear traditional clothing.

7 ___✗__ At night, families eat a big meal together to celebrate.

HW

D. *Write a paragraph about Jamhuri Day. Use the sentences on page 15.*

Jamhuri Day

Jamhuri Day is a patriotic holiday in Kenya. It takes place every December 12th. On this day in 1963, Kenya became an independent country. Kenyans have many ways to celebrate their freedom. People watch parades and play games in parks. Many Kenyans also wear traditional clothing on this day. At night families eat a big meal together to celebrate.

E. *Work with a partner. Read the topic sentence. Write three sentences that support it.*

Topic Sentence: We celebrate birthdays together in my family.

1. Its very important for us, we celebrated all families birdays

2. Birdays is not a big event in my Family, but we had a

3. I loved celebrate all birthays with a special dinner private party. made for me or my family goes to a restaurante, my children adults my

Building Word Knowledge

Words That Go Together. In your paragraph for this unit, you describe holidays and special events. Some *verbs + prepositions* "go together" to describe when these events happen. They help you answer the *When* question for your paragraph. Here are some examples.

take place + on (date)   *start/end +* at (time)   *last + for* (amount of time)
      in (month)   on (day)

*The Chinese New Year holiday **takes place in** January or February. This year, the holiday **starts on** February 2 and **ends on** February 8. It **lasts for** six days.*

It is = It's

A. Complete the sentences. Use words from the Building Word Knowledge box.

1. April Fool's Day ___takes place___ on April 1.

2. It ___lasts___ for a whole day.

3. It ___starts___ at 12:01 in the morning.

4. It ___ends___ at 12:00 noon.

→ your celebration (Thanksgiving)

B. Answer the questions about your assignment. Write complete sentences.

1. When does it take place?

   ___Thanksgiving Day takes place on the Fourth Thursday of November___

2. When does it start and end?

   ___It starts in the morning and ends after dinner.___
   Continues to this day.

3. How long does it last?

   ___It lasts all day long.___

   it last one day.

Tip for Writers

Capitalization. Capitalize the following words when you write about holidays and special events:

- the names of specific holidays and events
- months and days of the week
- the names of countries and towns

Here are some examples.

*In the **United States**, **Thanksgiving** is on the fourth **Thursday** in **November**.*
*We went to the **Chinese New Year** parade in **Taipei** last **February**.*

Circle the words that need capital letters.

1. The brazilian holiday carnival takes place in february or march.

2. On december 31, there is a big new year's eve celebration in new york city.

3. We celebrate teachers day on may 15.

4. In korea, we celebrate a traditional holiday with a parade.

Your Own Writing

Planning Your Body Sentences

A. *Look at your topic sentence on page 13. What information do you need to support your topic sentence? Check (✔) the questions you want to answer in your paragraph. Add other questions, if necessary.*

____✓____ Who celebrates the holiday or event?

____✓____ Why do people celebrate it?

____✓____ When does it take place?

____✓____ How long does it last?

____✓____ When does it start and when does it end?

____✓____ Where does it take place?

____✓____ What do people do? Do they have special clothing, music, or food?

Your own questions: _Do you celebrate this holiday?_

B. *Write your topic sentence. Write at least five supporting sentences to answer questions in Exercise A. Use your* wh- *questions chart and other information to help you.*

Topic Sentence: _Thanksgiven is the most important holiday in the USA._

- _People all over the Unite States celebrated Thankisgiven._
- _People celebrated it in memoria The First imigrants came from Engld._
- _It take place in Playmouth (mass)_
- _In Thankisgiven the famih made a big reunion and start together dinner._
- _We celebrated Thanks given in November._

C. **Checking in.** *Share your sentences with a partner. Discuss these questions.*

1. Which details support the controlling idea in the topic sentence?

2. Are there any details that do not support the controlling idea?

3. Which details are the most interesting?

4. Does your partner need to add more information to make anything clearer? What can your partner add?

After your discussion, do you want to rewrite your body sentences? Make changes to the sentences, if necessary.

■ THE CONCLUDING SENTENCE

The concluding sentence is usually the last sentence in the paragraph. It tells the reader that the paragraph is ending. The concluding sentence often repeats words or ideas from the topic sentence in a new way.

Example:

Topic Sentence: Teachers Day is a day to thank teachers for their hard work.

Concluding Sentence: Teachers help students a lot, so it is important to have a day to thank teachers.

Repeated Words: a day to thank teachers

Repeated Ideas: hard work → help students a lot

- Concluding sentences should *not* be about a different topic.

Incorrect concluding sentence: *We also celebrate Children's Day at my school.*

- Concluding sentences should *not* add a new detail.

Incorrect concluding sentence: *We also take class pictures with our teacher on Teachers Day.*

The Basic Paragraph
▶ Topic Sentence
▶ Body Sentences
▼ Concluding Sentence
• Repeat words or ideas from the topic sentence

Focused Practice

A. *Reread the paragraphs "New Year's Eve" on page 13, "Melbourne Cup Day" on page 14, and "Community Service Day" on page 15. Copy the concluding sentences. Then circle the words and ideas that are repeated from the topic sentences.*

1. New Year's Eve

Topic Sentence: New Year's Eve is a fun event in New York City.

Concluding Sentence: Everyone in time square is happy and has a good time on New year's Eve.

2. Melbourne Cup Day

Topic Sentence: Everything stops in Melbourne, Australia, for Melbourne Cup Day, a day everyone enjoys.

Concluding Sentence: Melbourne Cup Day is fun for all Australians.

3. Community Service Day

Topic Sentence: Community Service Day is a day to help other people in our community.

Concluding Sentence: We are all very tired, but we feel good because we helped other people.

B. *Read the paragraphs. Circle the best concluding sentence for each paragraph. Write it on the lines.*

Paragraph 1

The Running of the Bulls

    The Running of the Bulls (San Fermín) is an exciting event in Pamplona, Spain. It takes place every July in Spain. For one week, thousands of people go to the city of Pamplona. They wear red and white clothes, and dance and sing in the streets. They have parties all day and night. Then at 8:00 A.M., a group of bulls runs through the streets. Hundreds of people run in front of the bulls. The people stay away from the bulls. They run fast or stay close to the walls. Some people are slow or fall down, and they get hurt or killed. But most people are OK.

_____

_____

---

a. The San Fermín festival lasts for nine days.

b. No one is bored by the Running of the Bulls.

c. I think Pamplona is a beautiful city.

Paragraph 2

Vietnamese Rice-Cooking Contests

    Rice-cooking contests are traditional events in some parts of Vietnam. The contests take place during the Tet (New Year) festivals. Chefs compete to cook rice the traditional way—outside, over an open fire. It is not easy. For instance, the chefs often build fires in the wind and rain. In addition, they find and carry their own cooking water. In some competitions, chefs even work in small boats. As they cook rice, they are careful not to fall in the water or set the boat on fire.

_____

_____

---

a. I do not know how to cook rice the traditional way, but I like to eat it.

b. There are many other fun events during the Tet festivals.

c. The chef with the best rice wins the contest.

C. Work with a partner. Compare your concluding sentences for the paragraphs on page 20. Answer these questions.

1. What is the best concluding sentence for each paragraph? What words and ideas are repeated from the topic sentence?

2. Why are the other sentences incorrect concluding sentences? Which sentences add new details? Which sentences talk about different topics?

D. Work with a partner. Read the paragraph and write a concluding sentence. Repeat words or ideas from the topic sentence.

Our Super Birthday

My family has a fun tradition called "Super Birthday." A lot of people in my family have birthdays in May. My grandfather, my father, my mother, two of my brothers, my sister-in-law, and my niece were all born in May. It is difficult to have seven birthday parties in one month, so we have one big celebration instead. We have a big party for all our family and friends. We have a barbeque in the backyard, and get a giant cake. We put candles on the cake for each person, and everyone helps to blow them out.

We have a Fun Super Birthday every year its a great day for my Family.

HW

Your Own Writing

Planning Your Concluding Sentence

body sentences *21 concl.* *22 whole paragraph*

A. Read your topic sentence and supporting sentences on page 18. */13*

B. Write two or three important words from your topic sentence.

_____most_____ _____important_____ _____holiday_____

C. Write a concluding sentence that repeats the words or uses the words in a new way.

_____Thanksgiven is a great opportunite for everyone sey Thank you for all bleasing in your life._____

D. **Checking in.** Share your sentence with a partner. Did your partner . . .

• repeat two or three words or ideas from the topic sentence?

• use the words in different ways?

• write an interesting concluding sentence for the paragraph?

After your discussion, do you want to rewrite your concluding sentence? Make changes to the sentence, if necessary.

Writing Your First Draft

Write the first draft of your paragraph. Put your topic sentence, body sentences, and concluding sentence together in a paragraph. Give your paragraph a title. Hand in your first draft to your teacher.

Tip for Writers

Titles. Remember: Think about your audience—the people who will read your writing. A good title is one way to help prepare your readers to read the paragraph. A strong title clearly states the topic. A weak title is very general and does not give information about the topic. Here are some examples.

A weak title: *Danger and Excitement*

A strong title: *The Running of the Bulls*

A weak title: *A Day I Like*

A strong title: *A Day to Celebrate Teachers*

Read the titles. Check (✓) the three strongest titles.

_____ **1.** A Nice Day

___✓___ **2.** Children's Day

_____ **3.** A Celebration

___✓___ **4.** My Parents' Anniversary

_____ **5.** Cinco de Mayo (The Fifth of May)

_____ **6.** A National Holiday

Step 3 Revising

Revising your draft is another important step. Revising makes your writing better.

Revising means changing your writing. You revise when you have new ideas, information, or facts, or when you want to make your writing clearer. One way to make your paragraph clear is to use correct paragraph format.

Paragraphs in English have a special **format**. The paragraph format usually follows these rules:

- Indent (put a space before) the first sentence in a paragraph.
- Write one sentence after another on the same line, if possible.
- Start each sentence with a capital letter.
- End each sentence with a period.

Focused Practice

Look at the two paragraphs. Check (✓) the paragraph with the correct format. What are the mistakes in the incorrect paragraph? Discuss your answers with a partner.

☐ **Paragraph 1**

Old Home Day

Old Home Day is a traditional festival in Hancock, New Hampshire

It usually takes place in the summer.

For one weekend, people who grew up in the town come home. they play traditional games such as tug-of-war (two groups pull on different ends of a rope) and have pie-eating contests (people try to eat a pie really fast).

The people in town have a parade, wear costumes, and ride the town's fire trucks. In the evening, the firefighters make barbeque chicken, and there is an outdoor concert
old Home Day is a simple, old-fashioned holiday, but it is really fun.

☐ **Paragraph 2**

Old Home Day

Old Home Day is a traditional festival in Hancock, New Hampshire. It usually takes place in the summer. For one weekend, people who grew up in the town come home. They play traditional games such as tug-of-war (two groups pull on different ends of a rope) and have pie-eating contests (people try to eat a pie really fast). The people in town have a parade, wear costumes, and ride the town's fire trucks. In the evening, the firefighters make barbeque chicken, and there is an outdoor concert. Old Home Day is a simple, old-fashioned holiday, but it is really fun.

Your Own Writing

Revising Your Draft

A. *Reread the first draft of your paragraph. Use the Revision Checklist. What do you need to revise?*

B. *Revise your paragraph.*

Revision Checklist

Did you . . .

☐ describe a holiday or special event?

☐ include a topic sentence with a controlling idea?

☐ support the controlling idea with the body sentences?

☐ include a concluding sentence?

☐ repeat words from the topic sentence in the concluding sentence?

☐ use new vocabulary words from this unit?

☐ think about your audience and give information to your reader?

Step 4   Editing

■ GRAMMAR PRESENTATION

Before you hand in your revised paragraph, read it again and look for errors in grammar. In this section, you will review the simple present form. Think about your paragraph as you review.

Simple Present: Affirmative and Negative Statements

Grammar Notes	Examples
1. Use the **simple present** to tell about **things that happen again and again** (habits, regular occurrences, customs, and routines). **Now** Past —X—X—│—X—X—▶ Future *People dance on New Year's Eve.*	• I always **enjoy** my birthday. • We **go** to a restaurant to celebrate. • People **dance** on New Year's Eve.
2. Use the simple present to tell **facts**.	• The holiday **takes place** in December. • The party **starts** at 7:00 P.M.

3. In **affirmative statements**, use the **base form** of the verb for all persons except the third person singular. Add -**s** or -**es** with *he, she, it*.	• I **like** Jamhuri Day. • We **eat** traditional food. • People **play** traditional music. • He **eats** dinner with his family. • She **watches** the running of the bulls with friends.
4. In **negative statements**, use *do not* or *does not* before the base form of the verb.	• People **do not work** on New Year's Day. • My mother **does not stay** up until midnight.
5. The **third person singular affirmative** forms of **have**, **do**, and **go** are NOT <u>regular</u>. The **third person singular negative forms** of **have**, **do**, and **go** are <u>regular</u>.	• My school **has** a party. • My friend **does** a traditional dance. • He **goes** to the parade. • My school **does not have** a graduation party. • My friend **does not do** a traditional dance. • He **does not go** to the parade.
6. The verb **be** is **irregular**. It has three forms in the present: *is, am,* and *are*. In negative statements, use *not: is not, am not, are not*.	• I **am** at the parade. • The parade **is** fun. • My friends **are** with me. • My family **is not** with me.

Focused Practice

A. *Read the sentences. Circle the simple present verbs.*

1. Everyone in Australia watches the Melbourne Cup.

2. The parade begins at 12:00 P.M.

3. April Fool's tricks stop at noon.

4. People cook food outside and play games.

5. On Teachers Day, students thank their teachers for their hard work.

6. Everyone wears traditional clothes and dances and sings in the streets.

B. *Complete the paragraph with the simple present form of the verb.*

Alwyes
Sometimes
never
usually
every day
Twice a week
Routine

I
He
She
t Is

they
we
are

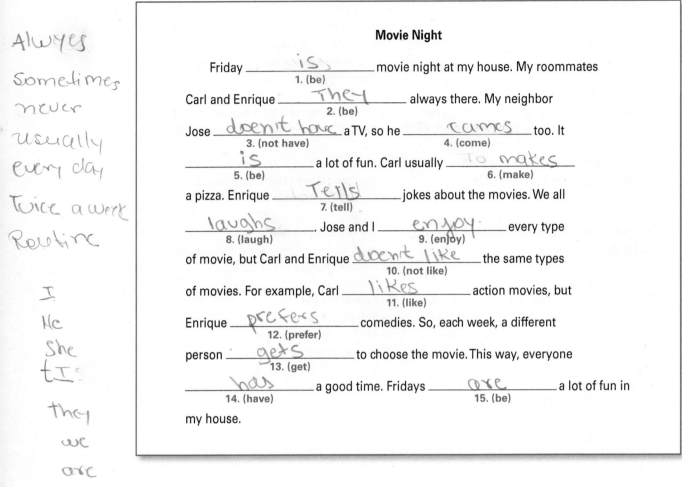

Movie Night

Friday ___is___ movie night at my house. My roommates
    1. (be)
Carl and Enrique ___They___ always there. My neighbor
    2. (be)
Jose ___doesn't have___ a TV, so he ___comes___ too. It
    3. (not have)   4. (come)
___is___ a lot of fun. Carl usually ___to makes___
    5. (be)   6. (make)
a pizza. Enrique ___tells___ jokes about the movies. We all
    7. (tell)
___laughs___. Jose and I ___enjoy___ every type
    8. (laugh)   9. (enjoy)
of movie, but Carl and Enrique ___doesn't like___ the same types
    10. (not like)
of movies. For example, Carl ___likes___ action movies, but
    11. (like)
Enrique ___prefers___ comedies. So, each week, a different
    12. (prefer)
person ___gets___ to choose the movie. This way, everyone
    13. (get)
___has___ a good time. Fridays ___are___ a lot of fun in
    14. (have)   15. (be)
my house.

C. *Read the paragraph. Correct six more simple present errors.*

Chuseok

                     is
      The Korean holiday Chuseok ~~are~~ a celebration of food and family. It take place
in autumn. People going back to their hometowns. They gathers in a relative's
house. Then, the fun begins. Everyone enjoy a big meal. People eating traditional
foods such as *songpyeon*, a type of rice cake, and *bulgogi*, a dish of meat and
vegetables. After dinner, people plays games and sing songs. Food and family are
important things, and that is why I like Chuseok.

D. *Write five sentences for your assignment. Use the simple present. They can be sentences you already have in your paragraph, or they can be new sentences.*

1. _____

_____

2. _____

_____

3. _____

_____

4. _____

_____

5. _____

_____

Your Own Writing

Editing Your Draft

A. *Edit your paragraph for the assignment. Use the Editing Checklist below.*

B. *Write a clean copy of your paragraph. Give it to your teacher.*

Editing Checklist
Did you . . .
☑ use the simple present correctly?
☑ use correct punctuation and capitalization?
☑ give your paragraph a title?
☑ format the paragraph correctly?

UH

UNIT 2 Everyday Heroes

IN THIS UNIT   You will write an opinion paragraph about a person you admire.

Martin Lee is just a regular person, but to his son Tommy, Martin is a hero. Martin spends time with Tommy every day. He helps Tommy with schoolwork and teaches him how to ride a bike. He gives him love and support. The world is full of everyday heroes like Martin. Who are the heroes in your life? What makes them heroes?

Planning for Writing

■ BRAINSTORM

A. *Read about Bethany Hamilton. What makes her a hero? Do you know other stories like this one? Discuss your answers with a partner.*

Bethany Hamilton Returns to the Ocean

Surfing is not easy. It is even more difficult with just one arm. Just ask Bethany Hamilton. At age 13, Bethany was surfing in Hawaii when a shark attacked her. Bethany lost her arm and almost died. Most people said, "She will never surf again." But Bethany was not afraid. Just one month after the attack, she returned to the ocean. She taught herself to swim and surf with one arm. It wasn't easy, but Bethany was hardworking and patient. She fell off her surf board many times, but she kept trying. After a lot of practice, she learned to surf again. Today, she is a champion surfer.

B. Using a Descriptive Wheel. You can use a descriptive wheel to help you get ideas for writing about a person you admire. In the middle of the wheel, you write the name of a person you admire. In the first circle, you write the qualities you admire in the person. For example, is the person intelligent, or strong? In the outside circle, you note examples of those qualities.

Work with a partner. Look at the descriptive wheel. Write the examples of Bethany Hamilton's qualities in the chart.

| She returned to the ocean. | She fell off but kept trying. | She is a champion surfer. |

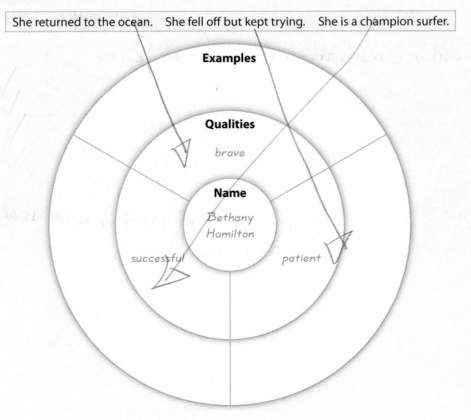

Examples

Qualities

brave

Name

Bethany Hamilton

successful   *patient*

Principal for a Day

1   It's Wednesday morning at Ashbury Middle School[1] in the town of Springfield, Ohio. Students are walking to class. Teachers are making lesson plans. A young boy is sitting in the principal's office. He is waiting. He misbehaved. The principal[2] is explaining the school rules to him. The boy is nervous, but so is Annie Hewitt, the principal. The reason? Today is Annie's first day as principal. And she's only 13 years old.

2   Annie won her school's "Principal for a Day" contest. For one day, Annie is in charge of[3] her school. She got the job because she is smart, hardworking, and popular. But to be successful as principal, she also needs to be tough.[4]

3   Annie's writing skills got her the job. Each year, Ashbury has an essay contest. Students write about why they should be principal. The teachers choose the winner. The idea came from Grover Smith, the school's real principal. He wanted to give students the chance to be a leader in their school. Annie doesn't remember everything she said in her winning essay, but "I do remember saying Mr. Smith needs a vacation," she laughs.

4   Mr. Smith knew Annie was a good choice. She had the qualities to be a good leader. As a student, Annie is hardworking and ambitious. She studies hard and gets good grades in her classes. The other students admire Annie. She was elected class president and has a lot of friends.

5   However, it is not enough to be popular. To succeed as principal, the other students must respect Annie. Students must listen to her and follow the school rules. For Annie, this is the most difficult part of the job. "Because I'm a kid . . . it's hard for me to be strict[5] with the other kids," she says. Annie felt bad after she punished the young boy in the morning.

6   At the end of the day, Annie says that she appreciates Mr. Smith more than before. She knows that a principal's job is not easy. Every moment there is something to do. The principal helps teachers, visits classrooms, talks with parents, plans school events, and much more. "It is really busy," she says.

7   Tomorrow, Mr. Smith will be in the principal's office again, and Annie will be in her classroom. Did she like being principal? "It was interesting," she says, "but I'm happy to be a regular student again tomorrow."

---

[1] **middle school:** a school for children in 6th through 8th grade (ages 10–14)
[2] **principal:** the director or head of a school
[3] **in charge of:** in control of or responsible for something
[4] **tough:** able to deal with difficult conditions
[5] **strict:** demanding that people obey rules

wH

Building Word Knowledge

Verbs for Admiration. There are several verbs that describe feelings about important or special people. Here are some examples.

• *admire* You *admire* someone when the person does something you think is good. You may want to be like the person.

*I **admire** my friend because he gets the highest grades in the class.*

• *respect* You *respect* someone when the person has good qualities or high standards. *Padros* You may or may not want to be like the person.

*I **respect** my brother because he is honest and kind.*

• *appreciate* You *appreciate* someone who is helpful or good to you. You may not like everything about the person.

*My math class is really hard, but I **appreciate** my teacher because I'm learning a lot.*

Circle the word that best completes each sentence. Discuss your answers with a partner.

Example:

Jim wants to be just like his father. He really (admires) / respects him.

1. Sarah does everything her father says. She really respects / appreciates him.

2. I admire / respect my father because he works 60 hours a week. I can't do that.

3. I appreciate / admire my brother because he helps me with my homework.

4. I want to be a famous singer like Shakira. I really admire / appreciate her.

5. He gave me a nice gift. I respect / appreciate it.

Focused Practice

A. *Read the article on page 30 again. Are these sentences True (T) or False (F)? Write T or F.*

___F___ 1. Annie Hewitt is the real principal of Ashbury Middle School. 1, 2, 3

___F___ 2. Grover Smith is Annie's teacher. 3

___T___ 3. Annie is popular and hardworking. 4

___F___ 4. Annie thinks that being a principal is an easy job. 6

B. *Circle the letter of the best way to complete each sentence.*

1. The young boy is in the principal's office because _____.

   a. he did something wrong /

   b. he gets good grades

   c. he is Annie's friend

(continued)

2. The purpose of the "Principal for a Day" program is to __3__.

   a. punish students

   (b.) teach students to be leaders

   c. give the principal a vacation

3. To be chosen as principal for a day, students must __5__.

   a. give a speech

   (b.) learn all the school rules

   c. win an essay contest

4. Annie's teachers think Annie __3__.

   a. does not like school

   b. needs to work harder in school

   (c.) is a good student

5. It is hard for Annie to punish her classmates because __5__.

   a. she is busy with other work

   b. they are the same age

   (c.) the school rules are hard

6. Annie learned that principals __C__.

   (a.) do a lot of work

   b. punish a lot of students

   c. have a lot of free time

C. *Work in a small group. Discuss your answers to the questions.*

   1. Do you think the "Principal for a Day" program is a good idea? Why or why not? *stude*

   2. What qualities does a person need to be a principal? *hardworking, ambitions, hard get good grades in class*

   3. Do you want to be a principal? Why or why not? *yes because it's a trehing you can be leorder.*

   4. Is the principal of a school an everyday hero? Why or why not?

Tip for Writers

Connecting Ideas with *Because*. Good writers use the word *because* to connect ideas in a sentence. *Because* answers the question *why*? Here are some examples.

Q: Why do you admire Bethany Hamilton?
A: She is brave.
*I admire Bethany Hamilton **because** she is brave.* *so young, persistent, olimist.*

Q: Why do you admire your father? *I don't.*
A: He works hard to support our family.
*I admire my father **because** he works hard to support our family.*

Don't forget the subject in the *because* clause.
I admire my sister **because she** *is a successful language learner.*

Use a pronoun (*he* or *she*) instead of repeating the person's name in the *because* clause.
I respect **Shakira** *because* ~~Shakira~~ *she is talented and generous.*

Combine the sentences with because.

1. **Q:** Why do you respect your uncle?

   A: He is intelligent and successful.

   I respect my uncle because he is intelligent and successful.

2. **Q:** Why do you appreciate your teacher?

   A: She is inspiring.

   I appreciate my teacher because she is inspiring.

3. **Q:** Why do you respect your principal?

   A: She is hardworking and kind.

   I respect my principal, because she is hardworking and kind.

4. **Q:** Why do you admire Lionel Messi?

   A: He is a talented athlete.

   I admire Lionel Messi, because He is a talented athlete.

5. **Q:** Why do you admire Lady Gaga?

   A: She writes creative songs.

   I admire Lady Gaga, because she writes creative songs.

Writing an Opinion Paragraph

In this unit, you are going to write an opinion paragraph. An opinion paragraph explains a personal belief or opinion. In your opinion paragraph, you will write about a person you admire. Like other paragraphs, an opinion paragraph has a topic sentence with a controlling idea, body sentences that support the topic sentence, and a concluding sentence.

> **The Opinion Paragraph**
> ▶ Topic Sentence
> ▶ Body Sentences
> ▶ Concluding Sentence

Step 1   Prewriting

Prewriting is an important step in the writing process. It helps you choose your topic and get ideas for your paragraph. In this prewriting, first you choose your assignment. Then you freewrite and use a descriptive wheel to help you get ideas for your writing.

Your Own Writing

Choosing Your Assignment

A. *Choose Assignment 1 or Assignment 2.*

Assignment 1: Write about someone you know well and admire. Describe the qualities that make you admire the person.

Assignment 2: Write about a celebrity or famous person you admire. Describe the qualities that make you admire the person.

B. *Think about the assignment. Write the names of people you admire next to the words below, or write your own list. Then choose one person to write about.*

People I Know Well	Celebrities or Famous People
Friend _Marco Aurelio N. Ses zeos_	TV personality _____
Parent _____	Actor _____
Family member _____	Businessperson _____
Teacher _____	Athlete _____
Your own idea _____	Your own idea _____

C. Freewriting is a way to get ideas about your topic. When you freewrite, you try to write down *all* your ideas. You do not think about whether the ideas are good or bad. You write any ideas that come into your mind. Later, you can choose ideas from your freewriting to use in your paragraph.

Freewrite for five minutes about the person you admire. Here are some questions to get you started.

- How do you know the person?

- What qualities do you admire?

- What are some examples of the qualities?

D. Checking in. *Share your ideas with a partner. Ask your partner questions and find out about your partner's person. For example:*

- Who is the person?

- What is the person like?

- Why do you admire this person?

After your discussion, add new ideas to your freewriting, if helpful.

E. *Complete the descriptive wheel for your assignment. Write the name of the person in the middle circle. Write three qualities you admire in the first circle. Then write examples of each quality in the outside circle.*

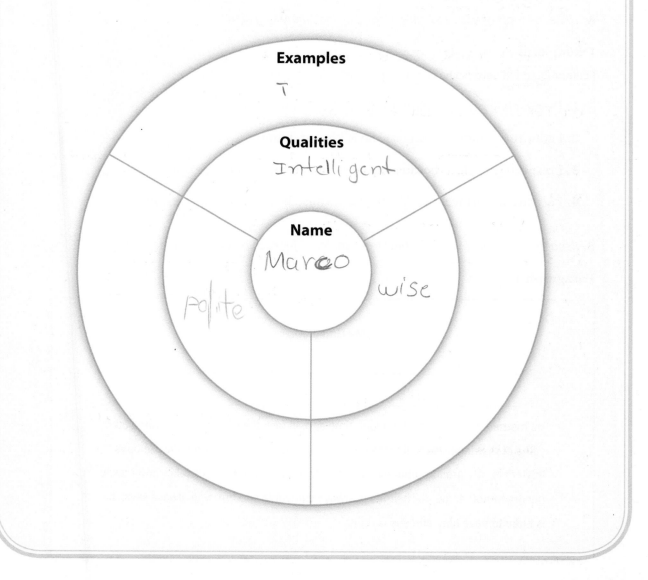

Examples

T

Qualities

Intelligent

Name

Mareo

wise

Polite

Step 2   Writing the First Draft

■ THE TOPIC SENTENCE

In Unit 1, you learned that the topic sentence has two parts: the topic and the controlling idea. In an opinion paragraph, the topic sentence tells the topic, and the controlling idea gives your opinion about the topic. For this assignment, the topic is the person you admire. The controlling idea is the reason or reasons you admire the person, that is, the qualities you admire in the person.

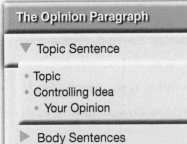

Example:

Topic Sentence: I admire my father because he is hardworking and dedicated to his family.

The **topic** is: my father

The **controlling idea (the qualities you admire):** hardworking and dedicated to his family.

Focused Practice

A. *Circle the topic of each sentence. Underline the controlling idea.*

Example:

I admire (Brad Pitt) because he is a successful actor and a generous person.

1. I appreciate (my grandfather) because he is intelligent.

2. I admire (my mother) because she is kind and funny.

3. I respect (Steve Jobs) because he is an influential businessperson.

4. I admire my art teacher, (Mr. Ikeda,) because he is creative and inspiring.

B. *Read the paragraph. Write the best topic sentence for each paragraph on the lines.*

Paragraph 1

My Grandfather

_____

_____

He married my grandmother a long time ago. In fact, they recently celebrated 50 years of marriage. After all these years, my grandfather is still romantic. He buys flowers for my grandmother every week. He is also funny. He tells jokes and makes my grandmother laugh. Their life is always enjoyable and fun. She always says she is lucky to have him, and she is right.

> The Opinion Paragraph
> ▼ Topic Sentence
> • Topic
> • Controlling Idea
>   • Your Opinion
> ▶ Body Sentences
> ▶ Concluding Sentence

a. I admire my grandfather because he teaches me a lot.

b. I admire my grandfather because he enjoys life.

c. I admire my grandfather because he is a great husband.

Paragraph 2

My Friend Caitlin

_____

_____

Caitlin is a great athlete. She always learns new sports. She skis, surfs, and skateboards. When she skis, she always tries the most dangerous mountains. She also tries many different types of food. Each week, she learns how to cook a new type of food. She also likes to go to new restaurants. One time, we went to a restaurant, and she ordered snake. I was too afraid to try it, but for a person like Caitlin, it was no problem.

---

a. I admire my friend Caitlin because she is a successful athlete.

b. I admire my friend Caitlin because she always tries new things.

c. I admire my friend Caitlin because she is hardworking and intelligent.

C. *Read the paragraph. Write a topic sentence. Discuss your topic sentence with a partner.*

My Uncle Ricardo

I admire my uncle Ricardo because he has a very dangerous job, but he never fells afraid.

My uncle is a firefighter. He has a very dangerous job, but he never feels afraid. brave
He goes into burning buildings to look for people. A few months ago, he saved a young boy's life. My uncle is also strong. He has to carry heavy equipment for his job. For example, a fire hose weighs almost 100 pounds. It is too much for me to carry, but for my uncle it is easy.

Your Own Writing

Finding Out More

A. *Go online. Type the keywords* **admirable people** *or* **people we admire** *or the name of your person. Find information about the person you admire or about admirable people in general.*

B. *Write notes about the* person. *For example, answer these questions.*

- Why do you admire these people?
- What words describe their qualities?
- What are some examples of these qualities?

Example:

Name: Brad Pitt

Qualities	Examples
generous	builds houses in New Orleans
humanitarian	helps people in Africa
kind	adopted three children
successful	starred in many movies (*Interview with a Vampire, Ocean's Eleven*)

Name: _Harriet Tubman_

Qualities	Examples
brave	she decided to be free and ran away from her owner.
Determined	she scape alone and across full and danger river
humanitarian	she help soldiers. be free, and she way spy foo USA.
daringle	her brothers' and husband here are very scared, but she runaway alone.

C. Checking in. *Share information with a partner. Did your partner . . .*

- explain why he or she admires this person?
- give examples of the person's qualities?
- talk about things you can use in your own writing?

After your discussion, add new ideas to your notes, if helpful.

Planning Your Topic Sentence

A. *Complete these sentences for your opinion paragraph. Use your descriptive wheel on page 35 and ideas from your notes above to help you.*

I admire _Harriet Tubman_ because _She was a humanitarian woman help soldiers and became spy._

I respect _Pres. Obama_ because _He was the first Black man became Pres. The USA._

I appreciate _my boss Corri_ because _She is generous and honest._

B. *Read your sentences in Exercise A. Choose the best topic sentence for your paragraph and answer these questions.*

1. What is the topic of your paragraph (the person you admire)?

Harriet Tubaman The brave slave woman.

2. What is the controlling idea (one or two qualities that make you admire this person)?

I admire Harriet Tubman because she had a strong personality and was brave.

■ THE BODY SENTENCES

The body sentences in a paragraph give important information to the reader. Remember: All the body sentences are about the controlling idea of the paragraph. They make the controlling idea in the topic sentence clear. In an opinion paragraph, the body sentences explain the writer's opinion. In this unit, they give examples to explain the qualities that you admire. An example can be something the person does or says, or it can be a detail that shows what other people think about the person.

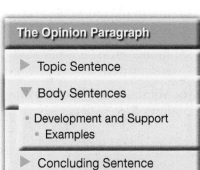

The Opinion Paragraph
▶ Topic Sentence
▼ Body Sentences
  • Development and Support
    • Examples
▶ Concluding Sentence

Example:

Shakira

I respect the singer Shakira because she is <u>talented</u> and <u>generous</u>. Shakira is a great singer and musician. She has many hit songs and music awards. She is from Colombia, but she is popular around the world. She has millions of fans. Shakira also has a big, generous heart. She is a (wealthy) woman, but she gives away a lot of her money. For example, she <u>built five schools for poor children in Colombia</u> because she wants all children to have a good education. She also <u>donates money</u> to give children a <u>good lunch at school</u>. Shakira is famous and successful, but she is not selfish, and I admire her a lot.

Prospera

The **topic** is: *Shakira*

The **opinion** (her qualities) is: *She is talented and generous.*

The **examples** for *talented* are:

- *Shakira is a great singer and musician.*
- *She has many hit songs and music awards.*
- *She is popular around the world.*

(continued)

The **examples** for *generous* are:

- *She gives away a lot of her money.*
- *She built five schools for poor children.*
- *She donates money to give children a good lunch at school.*

Focused Practice

A. *Read the sentences. Match the person's quality with the example.*

Quality ~~extrovertido~~

1. My father is (outgoing and friendly.)
2. Shakira is a popular singer.
3. Steve Jobs is an influential businessperson.
4. My English teacher is a great teacher.
5. Lionel Messi is a talented soccer player.
6. My sister is a hardworking lawyer.

Example

__3__ **a.** Every computer company tries to copy his ideas.

__5__ **b.** He is very fast and has great athletic skills.

__1__ **c.** He says hello to all the customers in his restaurant.

__2__ **d.** She has sold out concerts around the world.

__6__ **e.** She often works more than 60 hours per week at her law firm.

__4__ **f.** We have fun in her class, but we also learn a lot.

B. *Read the topic sentence. Check (✓) the examples that support the topic sentence.*

1. Topic Sentence: I admire J.K. Rowling because she is a great writer.

__✓__ **a.** She is very creative.

__✓__ **b.** J.K. Rowling is the author of the *Harry Potter* books.

_____ **c.** One day on a train, she had the idea for the *Harry Potter* story.

_____ **d.** J.K. Rowling is very generous.

_____ **e.** She gives money to hospitals.

__✓__ **f.** Her books are full of unusual characters with funny names.

2. Topic Sentence: I admire my friend (Chris) because he is <u>independent</u> and <u>adventurous</u>.

__✓__ **a.** Chris decided to see the world.

__✓__ **b.** He saved money so he could visit South America and Africa.

_____ **c.** He is a good cook.

_____ **d.** Chris can make any type of food.

__✓__ **e.** Chris did not travel with anyone.

__✓__ **f.** He visited 17 countries by himself.

It W.

C. *Read the paragraph. Write the opinion (the qualities that make the person admired) and the examples that support the opinion.*

Rachel McAdams

I respect Rachel McAdams because she is famous, but she acts like a regular person. Rachel McAdams is a Canadian actress. She is well-known for her movies. She is in popular movies like *The Notebook* and *The Time Traveler's Wife*. She won the MTV Movie Award and Teen Choice Award. However, she is also nice to her fans. One day my friend saw her at a café. She was friendly and talked with him for a while. She gave him her autograph and let him take her picture.

Quality 1: famous

Examples: she is well-know for her movie's, like The Notebook and the Times Travelers. Wife.

Quality 2: friendly

Examples: She talked with my Priend For a while, she gave him her autograh and let him take her picture.

Your Own Writing

Planning Your Body Sentences

A. *Look at your descriptive wheel on page 35, your topic sentence on page 39, and your notes. What qualities do you admire? Write examples to support your opinion of the person.* brave and

Topic Sentence: I admire Marco Aurelio because he was smart and intelligent.

Quality 1: Smart

Examples: He worked hard to have a legal career, he became a Justice promoter.

Quality 2: _intelligent_

Examples: _He is practical and quick when it comes to resolving conflicts._

B. Checking in. *Share your examples with a partner. Discuss these questions.*

1. Which examples best support the controlling idea in the topic sentence?

2. Are there any examples that do not support the controlling idea?

3. Which examples are the most interesting?

4. Do the examples help describe the person?

5. Does your partner need to add more information to make anything clearer? What can your partner add?

After your discussion, do you want to rewrite your body sentences? Make changes, if necessary.

■ THE CONCLUDING SENTENCE

The concluding sentence is the last sentence in the paragraph. It tells the reader that the paragraph is ending. In Unit 1, you learned that the concluding sentence often repeats words from the topic sentence. You can also restate ideas from the topic sentence. *Restate* means you say something in a different way. Instead of repeating the same words, use different words to say the same idea.

The Opinion Paragraph
▶ Topic Sentence
▶ Body Sentences
▼ Concluding Sentence
• Restate the topic sentence

Example:

Topic Sentence: I admire the singer Shakira because she is talented and generous.

Concluding Sentence: Shakira is famous and successful, but she is not selfish, so I admire her a lot.

Restated Ideas: talented → famous and successful; generous → not selfish

Building Word Knowledge

Synonyms. Synonyms are words or phrases that mean the same thing. Use synonyms to restate an idea in a new way. Here are some examples.

Adjective		Adjective
intelligent	=	smart
friendly	=	outgoing
considerate	=	thoughtful
rich	=	wealthy

Adjective		Verb Phrase
honest	=	tell the truth
supportive	=	support someone
talented	=	have talent
ambitious	=	have an ambition
kind	=	treat someone well
caring	=	care for someone
dedicated	=	dedicate oneself to something
inspiring	=	inspire someone

Restate the sentences. Use a synonym.

1. He is honest. He _is Trusty_ .

2. She is talented. She _has talent, she sing like a engel._

3. He is an ambitious filmmaker. He _works on Broadway_ to succeed in filmmaking.

4. He is a caring parent. He _takes good care of_ his children.

5. She is a dedicated employee. She _is dedicated_ herself to her work.

6. She is very thoughtful about other people's feelings. She _is considerate_ .

Focused Practice

A. *Read the topic sentences. Check (✓) the concluding sentence that restates the topic sentence.*

1. **Topic Sentence:** I admire my sister Ji Hyun because she is honest.

    Concluding Sentence:

    _✗_ **a.** Ji Hyun always tells the truth, so I admire her.

    _____ **b.** I admire Ji Hyun because she is nice to everyone.

    _____ **c.** Ji Hyun is a successful student because she works hard.

(continued)

2. Topic Sentence: I admire Nelson Mandela because he is an inspiring leader.

Concluding Sentence:

_____ **a.** Nelson Mandela was president of South Africa.

X **b.** Because Nelson Mandela inspires many people, he is my hero.

_____ **c.** Nelson Mandela is a great leader, so he has his own holiday.

3. Topic Sentence: I appreciate my boss because she treats the workers well.

Concluding Sentence:

_____ **a.** My boss works hard, so her employees respect her.

X **b.** Because my boss is rich and successful, I want to be like her.

X **c.** My boss is kind to her employees, so I like working for her.

B. *Work with a partner. Complete the concluding sentences. Restate the idea in the topic sentence. Use synonyms.*

1. Topic Sentence: I admire my mother because she dedicates herself to our family.

Concluding Sentence: Because my mother _devote your time_, I admire her.

2. Topic Sentence: I respect Microsoft founder Bill Gates because he is intelligent.

Concluding Sentence: Bill Gates _is very smart_, so I have a lot of respect for him.

3. Topic Sentence: I appreciate my boss because she is supportive of my career goals.

Concluding Sentence: Because my boss _encourage me in my goals_, I appreciate her so much.

4. Topic Sentence: I respect my brother Jawad because he is very honest.

Concluding Sentence: Jawad _is straight_, so I know that I can trust him.

C. *Reread the paragraph about Rachel McAdams on page 41. Copy the topic sentence below. Then write a concluding sentence. Restate the ideas from the topic sentence. Compare your sentence with a partner's.*

Topic Sentence: _I respect Rachel McAdams, because she is famous, but she acts like a regular person._

Concluding Sentence: _Rachel McAdams really is kind, so I have respect for her._

4W

Your Own Writing

Planning Your Conclusion

A. *Write your topic sentence from page 39. Write a concluding sentence that restates your topic sentence.*

Topic Sentence: I respect and admire Harriet Tubman because was brave to escape alone to Freedom, Freed more than Three hundred slaves as she had a strong personality.

Concluding Sentence: Harriet Tubman inspires me to make the thinks different and better.

B. **Checking in.** *Share your topic sentence and concluding sentence with a partner. Discuss these questions.*

1. Does the concluding sentence restate the idea in the topic sentence with synonyms?

2. If yes, which words restate the ideas in the topic sentence?

3. If no, how can you restate the ideas?

After your discussion, do you want to rewrite your concluding sentence? Make changes to the sentence, if necessary.

Writing Your First Draft

Write the first draft of your paragraph. Put your topic sentence, body sentences, and concluding sentence together in a paragraph. Give your paragraph a title. Hand in your first draft to your teacher.

Step 3   Revising

Revising your draft is another important step. Revising makes your writing better. Revising means changing your writing. You revise when you have new ideas, information or facts, or when you want to make your writing clearer. You may need to change, add or delete words or sentences, or move sentences to a different place in the paragraph.

Tip for Writers

Clauses with *Because*. The clause with *because* can come at the beginning or end of a sentence. When *because* is at the beginning of a sentence, put a comma after the *because* clause. Here are some examples.

I admire my brother **because he is honest**.

Because he is honest, *I admire my brother.*

Rewrite your concluding sentence. Begin with **Because.**

Because Harriet Tubman is brave and she had a strong personality I admire her.

HW

Focused Practice

A. *Read the paragraph.*

My Father

    I appreciate my father because he is hardworking and dedicated to his family. My father owns a Vietnamese restaurant in Los Angeles. He works at the restaurant all the time. On most days, he goes to the restaurant at 10:00 A.M. and leaves after it closes at night. He does many different jobs. He greets the customers when they come in, manages the staff, and does the accounting. However, he also takes care of our family. He's very busy, but he still helps my sister and me with our homework. He calls us from the restaurant every day after school. He cares about our feelings, and we can always ask him for advice. Because of my father's love and hard work, I appreciate him more every day.

B. *Work with a partner. Answer the questions about the paragraph.*

1. What is the topic of the paragraph? Circle it.
2. What is the controlling idea of the paragraph? Underline it.
3. What examples support the controlling idea? How many are there? _____
4. What words in the concluding sentence restate words in the topic sentence? Circle them.

Your Own Writing

Revising Your Draft

A. *Reread the first draft of your paragraph. Use the Revision Checklist. What do you need to revise?*

B. *Revise your paragraph.*

Revision Checklist

Did you . . .

☑ describe someone you admire, respect, or appreciate?

☑ include a topic sentence with a controlling idea?

☑ support the controlling idea with the body sentences?

☑ restate the ideas from the topic sentence in your concluding sentence?

☑ use *because* to explain your ideas?

GRAMMAR PRESENTATION

Before you hand in your revised paragraph, read it again and look for errors in grammar, capitalization, and punctuation. In this section you will review descriptive adjectives. Think about your paragraph as you review.

Descriptive Adjectives

Grammar Notes	Examples
1. Adjectives describe nouns.	noun adjective • My **cousin** is **talented**. adjective noun • She is a **talented dancer**.

2. Adjectives can come
  • after the verb **be**.
  • before a noun.
	
	• My brother *is* **honest**.
	• He is an **honest** *person*.
	  NOT: He is a person honest.

3. Do **NOT** add **-s** to an adjective.	• *The Alchemist* is a **great** book. • Paulo Coelho writes **great** books. NOT: Paulo Coelho writes greats books.

4. For **adjective + noun:**
  • Use **a** if the adjective begins with a **consonant sound**.
  • Use **an** if the adjective begins with a **vowel sound**.
	
	• She is **a s**upportive teacher.
	
	• She is **an i**nspiring teacher.

5. Some adjectives end in **-ing**, **-ly**, or **-ed**.	• She is **interesting**. • He is **friendly**. • She is **dedicated**.

6. When you connect two ideas with *and*:
  • Connect **two adjectives** after *be*.
  • Connect **two adjective + noun phrases**.
	
	• My father is **successful** and **caring**.
	• My father is **a successful businessperson** and **a loving father**.
	  NOT: My father is successful and a loving father.

Focused Practice

A. *Read the sentences. Circle the adjectives.*

1. The president is an (inspiring) leader. ✓
2. His speeches are (interesting). ✓
3. He makes (important) decisions for the country. ✓
4. My cousin is a (successful) businessperson. ✓
5. His job is (exciting) and (challenging). ✓
6. He takes (expensive) vacations. ✓

B. *Use the words to write a sentence. Remember: Use capital letters to begin a sentence and a period to end the sentence.*

Example:

lawyer / brother / a / hardworking / my / is

My brother is a hardworking lawyer.

1. talented / writer / a / Paulo Coelho / is

   Paulo coelho is a talented writer. ✓

2. are / books / interesting / his

   His books are interesting. ✓

3. a / Mark Zuckerburg / businessperson / successful / is

   Mark Zuckerburg is a seccessful businessperson. ✓

4. rich / he / and / famous / is

   He is famous and rich. ✓

5. fast / Liu Zige / is / swimmer / a

   Liu Zige is a fast swimmer. ✓

6. she / world record / new / set / a

   In 2008, she set a new world record. ✓

C. *Read the paragraph. Correct four more adjective errors.*

My Friend Raul

I admire my friend Raul because he is an successful artist. His parents told him not to be an artist, but he did not listen. At first, he did not sell many paintings, but today his work is well known. Raul is a painter talented. His work is creative and beautiful. His paintings are in several importants museums. Raul is also a person hardworking. He spends all day in his art studio. Because Raul is successful, I think I can be a successful too.

D. *Write five sentences for your assignment. Use adjectives in your sentences. They can be sentences you already have in your paragraph, or they can be new sentences.*

1. Harriet is a brave woman to escape alone From Freedom
2. Tubman is a humanitarian woman who Freed more than 300 th. slaves
3. She had a strong personality.
4. Teacher Alice is a beautiful and smart woman.
5. The students are very interted in proving There English

Your Own Writing

Editing Your Draft

A. *Edit your paragraph for the assignment. Use the Editing Checklist below.*

B. *Write a clean copy of your paragraph. Give it to your teacher.*

Editing Checklist

Did you . . .

- ☑ use adjectives correctly?
- ☑ punctuate sentences correctly?
- ☑ give your paragraph a title?
- ☐ format the paragraph correctly?
- ☐ use new vocabulary words from this unit?

UNIT 3 Turning Points

IN THIS UNIT You will write a narrative paragraph about a turning point in someone's life.

ponto de virada

A turning point is an event that changes a person's life. Every life has turning points. For some people, it is graduating from school. For others, it is getting married or having children. We usually remember these events for a long time. What other events can be turning points? What events will you always remember?

■ BRAINSTORM

A. *Read an article about Susan Boyle. What was the turning point in her life? Discuss your answers with a partner.*

I Dreamed a Dream

Susan Boyle had a quiet life in Blackburn, Scotland. She lived at home and took care of her mother. She loved to sing, and she sometimes performed in her village.

In 2007, Susan's mother died. Before she died, Susan made a promise to her mother. She promised to audition[1] for the TV show *Britain's Got Talent*.

In 2009, Susan had her audition. At first, the audience laughed at her. But then she started to sing, and everyone was amazed by her beautiful voice. The audience stood and cheered.

Ten million people watched Susan perform on TV. In the next nine days, 100 million more people watched her on the Internet. Later that year, she recorded her first album. It sold more than 9 million copies.

_____

[1] **audition:** to give a short performance that is judged

B. **Using a Timeline.** When you tell a story, you can use a timeline to organize your ideas. A timeline shows the order of events in the story, from first to last.

Work with a partner. Put the events in "I Dreamed a Dream" in order on the timeline, from first to last.

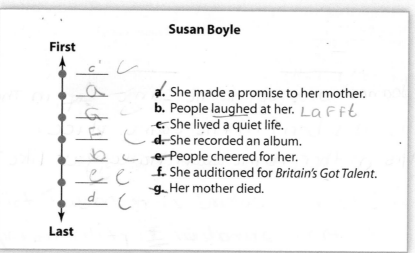

Susan Boyle

First

- c
- a
- g
- f
- b
- e
- d

a. She made a promise to her mother.
b. People laughed at her. Lafft
c. She lived a quiet life.
d. She recorded an album.
e. People cheered for her.
f. She auditioned for *Britain's Got Talent*.
g. Her mother died.

Last

■READ

Read the article about a turning point in someone's life.

Across the Street, a Long-Lost Brother

1   Tara Rivers always knew she had a brother. She did not know his name. She did not know his address. She did not even know what he looked like, but she searched for him anyway. And in 2010, she finally found him. He lived right across the street.

2   The story begins on August 22, 1978. On that day, Tara's mother Marie gave birth to a baby boy. Marie was just 16 years old. She was scared and confused. She loved the baby very much, but she was young and she did not know how to be a mother. She decided to give the boy up for adoption.[1] She was sad, but it was the best thing for the baby.

3   Years went by. Marie had two more children, but she never forgot her first child. She worried about her son, so she decided to search for him. However, she could not find him.

4   In 2009, Tara joined her mother's search. She was curious about her brother. She was interested in finding him, but after 32 years, she had little hope. Then Tara had the conversation that changed her life.

5   One sunny afternoon, Tara saw her neighbor Lance, and they chatted. "When's your birthday?" she asked. "August 22," Lance said. Tara was surprised. Then she asked another question. "What year were you born?" She did not believe the answer. Lance was born the same day, in the same year, and in the same place as her long-lost brother. Was it possible?

6   Lance ran inside his house. He phoned his adoptive parents.[2] "What was my birth mother's[3] name?" he asked. They only knew her first name, but it was Marie, just like Tara's mother. Lance and Tara now felt certain that they were brother and sister, but they had to be sure.

7   Lance decided to take a DNA[4] test. The test could show if he was related to Marie and Tara. For weeks, they nervously waited for the results.

8   On February 5, 2010, the answer came in the mail. Marie, Tara, and Lance's adoptive parents were there. Lance held the envelope. His hands shook. Then he opened the letter and saw the news. The test showed that Marie was Lance's mother.

9   It was a happy moment for everyone. Marie hugged her son and cried. Lance thought about his future. "It's like a new beginning," he said. Lance's adoptive parents were happy for him. Their son found his long-lost family. Lance was excited about it too. He found more than a mother and sister. He found himself.

---

[1] **give up for adoption:** to legally allow your child to become part of another family
[2] **adoptive parents:** parents who adopt a child
[3] **birth mother:** a woman who has a baby, but does not raise the child
[4] **DNA:** genetic information in your cells

Building Word Knowledge

Words that Go Together. Some verbs and adjectives are often followed by a specific preposition. It is important to learn the word and preposition together so that you can use them correctly. Here are some examples.

Verb + Preposition

search   for

• Tara **searched for** her brother.

Adjective + Preposition

curious   about

• Tara was **curious about** her brother.

Find the preposition combinations in the article on page 52. Write the preposition. Write the sentence from the article.

1. Verb + Preposition

a. worry ___about___

She worried about her son,

b. wait ___For___

For weeks, They nervously waited For the results.

c. think ___about___

Lance thought about his Future.

2. Adjective + Preposition

a. interested ___in___

She was interested in Finding him,

b. related ___to___

The test could show if he were related to Marie and Tara.

c. happy ___For___

Lance's adoptive parents were happy For him.

d. excited ___about___

Lance was excited about i too

Focused Practice

A. *Read the article on page 52 again. Write the events from the story in the timeline.*

5 Lance asked his adoptive parents about his birth
   mother.

7 Lance found out that Marie is his mother.

6 Lance took a DNA test.

2 Marie decided to search for her son.

1 ✓ Marie gave her son up for adoption.

4 Tara had a conversation with her neighbor, Lance.

3 Tara helped her mother search for her brother.

First

1 On August 22, 1978 — *Marie gave her son up for adoption.* _____

2 _____

In 2009 — 3 _____

4 _____

5 _____

6 _____

On February 5, 2010 — 7 _____

Last

B. *Tara chatted with Lance and thought he was her brother. Why? Write the reasons.*

1. *He was born on August 22.* _____

2. Lance was born the same day, in the same year

3. He was born in the same place.

4. His mother name was Marie, just like Tara's mother.

Foggy

C. *Make inferences (good guesses) about Marie and Lance. Discuss your answers with a small group.*

1. How did Marie probably feel after she gave Lance up for adoption? She was sad, worried. (4)
2. Why did Marie decide to search for her son? because she never forgot her first child. (3,4)
3. Why did Lance's hands <u>shake</u> when he opened the DNA test results? He was excited.
4. Why were Lance's adoptive parents happy about the results of the DNA test? because their son found his long-lost family.
5. What did Lance mean when he said, "It's like a new beginning"? What does "He found himself" mean? It's like a new beginning, because now he had a new family, he know how are his mother and relatives.

Tip for Writers
He found himself mean, now he can know his family history, he

Joining Ideas with *And*, *But*, and *So*. When you tell a story, you can join ideas using the coordinating conjunctions *and, but,* and *so*. Use a comma before the conjunction.

• *And* joins two similar ideas.

• *But* introduces a contrast or opposite idea.

• *So* introduces a result.

Here are some examples.

*Tara saw her neighbor Lance, **and** they chatted.* Conversam

*She loved the baby very much, **but** she was young.*

*She worried about her long-lost son, **so** she decided to search for him.*

Complete each sentence with and, but, *or* so.

1. Tara wanted to find her brother, ___but___ she did not know his name.
2. Lance's birthday was August 22, ___and___ his birth mother was named Marie.
3. Lance and Tara wanted to be sure, ___so___ they took a DNA test.
4. Lance's adoptive parents were happy, ___and___ Lance was happy too.
5. Marie cried, ___but___ she was not sad.

Writing a Narrative Paragraph

In this unit, you are going to write a narrative paragraph about a turning point or memorable event in someone's life. A narrative paragraph tells a story. All the sentences in the paragraph work together to tell the story in order, from beginning to end.

> **The Narrative Paragraph**
>
> ▶ Topic Sentence
> ▶ Body Sentences
> ▶ Concluding Sentence

Step 1 Prewriting

Prewriting is an important step in the writing process. It helps you choose your topic and get ideas for your paragraph. In this prewriting, first you choose your assignment and topic. Then you write and discuss ideas about your topic, and make a timeline to help you order the events in your narrative paragraph.

Your Own Writing

Choosing Your Assignment

A. *Choose Assignment 1 or Assignment 2.*

Assignment 1: Write a story about a turning point in your life or someone else's life.

Assignment 2: Write a story about a memorable event in your life or someone else's life.

B. *Look at the list of turning points and memorable events. Check (✓) possible turning points or memorable events for your assignment and add your own ideas. Then choose one to write about.*

Turning Points and Memorable Events

_____ start school   _____ move to a new place

_____ graduate from school   _____ make a friend

_____ travel   _____ get married

_____ learn something new   _____ your own ideas

_____ win a contest   _____

_____ get in an accident   _____

✓ find a job

C. Freewriting is a way to get ideas about your topic. Freewriting is different than just thinking about a topic. When you write your ideas on paper, you can look at them again later. Writing can also help you think of new ideas. When you freewrite, you try to write down all your ideas. Later, you can choose which ideas to use in your paragraph.

Freewrite for five minutes about a turning point or memorable event. Don't worry about grammar or spelling. Just write down all your ideas. Here are some questions to get you started.

• Why is this event memorable or a turning point?

• Who did it happen to?

• When and where did it happen?

D. **Checking in.** *Share your ideas with a partner. Ask your partner questions about the story of the memorable event or the turning point. For example:*

• Who is the story about?

• What happened?

• Why was the event important or memorable?

After your discussion, add new ideas to your freewriting.

E. *Complete a timeline for your story. Write the name of the turning point or memorable event. List the events from first to last.*

Event: A Turning point in my llfe was when I got
First married and had my babys.

1994 I was 24 years old when I meet with my
husband in 1994.

1995 Jones and I got engaged, I was 26 years old
and he 28, we lived in Belo Horizonte, MG

1996 we got marriend and moved to Curitiba. Pr

1997 My first child was born I was 27 year old
and my husband started studying in univer
sity.

2021 I had my last child, I'm a mother of three
Last boys and one girl. I've been married for
26 years.

■ THE TOPIC SENTENCE

A narrative paragraph tells a story. The topic sentence (introduces) the story to the reader. A good topic sentence will make the reader interested. It makes the reader want to read the story and find out: What happened? Why was the story important?

In this assignment, the topic sentence should answer one of these questions:

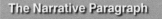

The Narrative Paragraph

▼ Topic Sentence
  • Topic
  • Controlling Idea
    • Introducing the Story

▶ Body Sentences
▶ Concluding Sentence

• Why was the event memorable?

• Why was the event a turning point in the person's life?

Example:

Topic Sentence: A boat ride to Kowloon changed my life forever.

The **topic** is the event: A boat ride to Kowloon

The **controlling idea** is the reason the event was important: It changed my life forever.

This topic sentence invites the reader into the story. It makes the reader interested in reading more and finding out more about the event.

Focused Practice

A. *Read the topic sentences. Write the topic (the event) and the controlling idea (why the event was memorable or was a turning point).*

Example:

Topic Sentence: The best day of my life was the day my soccer team won the championship.

Topic: The day my soccer team won the championship.

Controlling Idea: the best day of my life

1. A mountain climbing trip changed my friend Elena's life.

   Topic: the trip changed my friend Elenas' life

   Controlling Idea: My friends Elena's life changed

2. My high school graduation was an exciting day for me.

   Topic: My high school graduation

   Controlling Idea: exciting day for me.

3. My first trip to Japan was a trip I will always remember.

   Topic: My first trip to Japan

   Controlling Idea: a trip I will always remember

4. My father quit smoking and became happier and healthier.

Topic: _My Father quit smoking._

Controlling Idea: _He became happier and healthier._

5. A visit to an art museum was life-changing for my sister.

Topic: _A visit to an art museum._

Controlling Idea: _was life-changing for my sister_

6. My grandmother's death was a turning point in my life.

Topic: _My grand mother's death_

Controlling Idea: _It's was a turning point in my life_

B. *Read the narrative paragraphs. Check (✓) and write the topic sentence that includes both the topic (the event in the story) and the controlling idea (why the event was memorable or was a turning point). Compare your answers with a partner.*

Paragraph 1

A Frightening Car Accident

My friend borrowed his parents' car, we
had an interstate relaxing later but we had a car accident. how I
try to drive more carefully.

My friend borrowed his parents' car because we wanted to go to the beach. We
left early in the morning. We got to the beach safely, and had a nice, relaxing
day. On the way home, my friend was tired from the sun. Then, it started to rain.
Suddenly, the car went off the road. The car rolled over and stopped upside down.
Fortunately, we had our seat belts on, so we were not badly hurt. The police
and ambulance came and took us to the hospital anyway. After that frightening
experience, I try to drive more carefully.

_____ **a.** Car accidents are very frightening.

_____ **b.** I was in a car accident a few years ago.

_____ **c.** Many people are hurt each year in car accidents.

__✓__ **d.** The most frightening event in my life was a car accident last year.

scary

Paragraph 2

The Turning Point in My Father's Life

_____

_____

For 15 years, my father worked as a furniture salesperson. Then he lost his job because his company had financial problems and had to close. My father looked for a new job, but he did not find one. After a few months, he decided to go back to school. He studied computer repair. Then he opened a computer repair shop. At first, business was not good. After a while, he got more customers. Soon, he was working full-time. Today, he is his own boss, and the business is making money. In the end, my father is happier today with his new career.

_____ **a.** My father worked hard for many years, but then he lost his job.

_____ **b.** A lot of people lost their jobs because of the world economic crisis.

✓ **c.** My father lost his job, but he found a new career and a new life.

_____ **d.** My father's company went out of business.

C. _Read the paragraph. Write a topic sentence. Be sure to include the topic (the event in the story) and the controlling idea (why the event was memorable or was a turning point for the writer)._

A Change of Plans

The filmmaking class changed my plans for future.

In my last year in high school, I had time for an extra class. There were only two classes available: French and filmmaking. I spoke French already, so I took the filmmaking class. I did not know anything about making films. Soon, I discovered that I really liked it. I liked filming, and I liked editing the film later. For the final project, I made a film about my neighborhood. My teacher thought the film was very good. She encouraged me to send it to a film contest for high school students. My film won third place in the contest. After this experience, I decided to study filmmaking in college. In the end, the filmmaking class changed my plans for the future.

Your Own Writing

Finding Out More

A. *Go online. Type the keywords* won a championship, met my wife, got a scholarship, my graduation, *or the name of your event. Find information and stories about a similar turning point or memorable event. Look for new words and new ideas for your paragraph.*

B. *Answer the questions. Take notes.*

1. How does the story begin?

_____

2. What words make the story interesting?

_____

3. Does the story have a beginning, middle, and end?

_____

4. What happened? Why was it a turning point or a memorable event?

_____

5. Is the story similar to your story? How is it similar? How is it different?

_____

C. **Checking in.** *Share your information with a partner. Did your partner . . .*

- find interesting stories?
- learn new words and new ideas?
- find a similar story to the story for the assignment?
- offer any ideas you can use in your writing?

After your discussion, add new ideas to your story, if helpful.

Planning Your Topic Sentence   *HW*

A. *Write two topic sentences for your paragraph. Use your timeline on page 57, your freewriting, and the information above to help you. Circle the topic and underline the controlling idea in each sentence.*

A Turning point in my life was when I got married.

I got married when I was 27 years old. I've been married for 26 years.

B. *Choose one of your topic sentences for your paragraph. Write the sentence.*

Topic Sentence: A Turning point in my life was when I got married, I _____

HW

Tip for Writers

Writing a Controlling Idea. In this unit, a strong controlling idea tells the reader why an event was memorable or a turning point. Some phrases can help you express these ideas. Here are some examples.

- *changed my life (or someone else's life) forever*

A mountain climbing trip **changed my friend Elisa's life forever**. ✓

- *was an exciting (or sad or happy) day for me (or someone else)*

My high school graduation **was an exciting day for me**.

- *is something I (or someone else) will always remember*

My first trip to Japan **was a trip I will always remember**. ✓

- *was a life-changing event (or turning point in my life)*

My grandmother's death **was a turning point in my life**.

- *taught me (or someone else) an important lesson*

A frightening car accident **taught my friend an important lesson**.

Rewrite your topic sentence three different ways. Use the phrases above to express the controlling idea.

1. When I got marriend 26 year ago my lifed changec forever.

2. After my wedding ceremony I moved for my husband's citic I will always remember that memorable day.

3. A turning point in my life was when I got married.

■ THE BODY SENTENCES

The body sentences form the largest part of a paragraph. In the body of a paragraph, you develop and support the controlling idea in your topic sentence. Remember: All the body sentences are about the one topic and the controlling idea.

In a narrative paragraph, the body sentences tell a story. They often describe the events in order, starting with the first event and ending with the last event.

The Narrative Paragraph
▶ Topic Sentence
▼ Body Sentences
• Development and Support
• Time Order
• Background
▶ Concluding Sentence

Time Order

In a narrative paragraph, the reader should experience the story as it happens. Usually you write about the events in the story in time order. You start with the first event, describe the following events, and end with the last event. Time words help order the events in a story.

Time Words: Specific Date or Time	Time Words: A Sequence of Events
In May 2008	after that
a few weeks later	the next day
one day	soon
on the first day	then
in the morning	later
now	finally

Example:

A Ferry Ride to Kowloon

A ferry ride to Kowloon changed my life forever. In June 1998, I was in Hong Kong with my friend Chen. On the last day of the trip, we planned to go sightseeing in Kowloon, but in the morning, Chen felt sick. He wanted to stay in the hotel, so I decided to go by myself. I went to the ferry terminal and got my ticket. It was a sunny day, so I sat on the top deck of the ferry. Then a young woman sat next to me, and we started talking. Her name was Jing. She was on her way to work at a Kowloon hotel. After the one-hour trip, we felt like best friends. We emailed each other for months afterwards. The next summer, I visited her again. Now, she is my wife.

The events in the story are in order, from first to last. Time words help the reader understand when an event happened in the story.

The time words describe the dates and times:
in June 1948, on the last day, in the morning

The time words describe the sequence of events in the story:
after the one-hour trip, the next summer, now

Focused Practice

A. *Read the paragraph. Circle the topic and underline the controlling idea in the topic sentence. Then underline the time words in the paragraph.*

An Unexpected Meeting

An unexpected meeting with a teacher was the turning point in Hilda Solis's life. Hilda's family was poor. Her parents worked in a factory, and she had seven brothers and sisters. In high school, Hilda had little hope for her future. College was expensive, so she planned to work as a secretary in an office. One day, close to graduation, she saw her history teacher, Mr. Sanchez, and told him about her plans. Mr. Sanchez was disappointed. Hilda was smart, and he wanted her to go to college. The next week, with Mr. Sanchez's help, Hilda filled out the college applications. A few months later, a college in California accepted her and gave her a full scholarship to pay for her education. Many years later, Hilda did become a secretary—but not in an office. In 2009, she became the U.S. secretary of labor. Today, she helps millions of Americans find jobs. Without Mr. Sanchez, Hilda's life might be very different.

B. *Read the paragraph in Exercise A again. Put the events in order. Number the events from 1 (first event) to 6 (last event).*

___6___ **a.** Hilda became the U.S. secretary of labor.

___5___ **b.** Hilda got a full scholarship to college.

___2___ **c.** Hilda planned to be a secretary in an office.

___3___ **d.** Hilda talked to her teacher, Mr. Sanchez, about her plans.

___1___ **e.** Hilda was a high school student.

___4___ **f.** Mr. Sanchez helped Hilda apply for college.

C. *Complete the sentences. Use the time words. Remember: Use capital letters, if necessary.*

1. at first / finally

Learning to play tennis was difficult. ___At First___ I missed the ball all the time, but I kept trying. ___finally___, I started to play better.

2. the next day / in March 2006

o Fora do país.

I arrived in Sydney ___in March 2006___ for a year abroad. My host family

picked me up at the airport. ___The next day___, I started my new school.

3. after that / first

Graduation day was very exciting. ___first___, we listened to

the graduation speeches. ___After___, we got in a line to get our

diplomas.

4. two days later / on May 23

___On May 23rd___, my daughter was born. We took her home from the

hospital ___two days later___.

5. first / then

My brother traveled in Asia after college. ___first___, he traveled

through China. ___Then___, he visited Japan.

6. now / last year

___Last year___, I was in a terrible car accident.

___Now___, I am afraid to drive.

D. _Read the topic sentence. Number the sentences in order from 1 (first event) to 6 (last event). Use the time words to help you. Then write the paragraph with the sentences in order._

1. Topic Sentence: Justin Bieber put his videos on YouTube, and his life was never the same.

___3___ **a.** At age 12, Justin entered a local talent contest in Canada. He came in second in the contest.

___2___ **b.** He started to sing at age 3. Later, he taught himself to play a guitar, a piano, and a drum set.

___4___ **c.** His family and friends did not see his performance in the talent contest, so his mother posted the video on YouTube.

___5___ **d.** Soon, thousands or people started watching Justin's videos each day. Then the singer Usher heard his music and helped him make his first record, _My World_.

___6___ **e.** Today, Justin Bieber is an international star because of his online videos.

___1___ **f.** As a baby, Justin played drums on his mother's pots and pans.

quando

(continued)

HW

As a baby, Justin played drums on his mother's pots and pans. He started to sing at age 3. Later he taught himself to play a guitar, a piano, and a drum set. He started to sing at age 3. Later he taught himself to play a guitar, a piano, and drum set. His family and friends did not see his performance in the talent contest, so his mother posted the video on Youtube. (5, 6)

2. Topic Sentence: The best day of my life was the day my soccer team won a championship.

_3_ **a.** At first, the other team got a goal, and my team did not score.

_5_ **b.** In the last minute of the game, I got the ball, ran up the field, and kicked the ball. It flew past the goalie and into the goal.

_1_ **c.** On the day of the game, the soccer stadium was full. My family was there and so were a lot of my friends.

_6_ **d.** The game was over, and my team won! For one day, I was the hero, and everyone loved me.

_2_ **e.** The soccer players came onto the field, and then the game began.

_4_ **f.** Then in the second half, my team scored a goal, so the game was tied one-one.

On the day of the game, the soccer stadium was full. My family was there and so were a lot of my friends. The soccer players came onto the field, and then the game began. At first, the other team got a goal, and my team did not score. Then in the second half, my team scored a goal, so the game was tied one-one. (5, 6)

Background Information

The body of the paragraph may also give background information. Background information usually comes at the beginning of a paragraph. Background information makes the story more interesting. It also helps the reader understand the story. For example, you can choose background information to

- explain when and where the story happened.
- describe important events that happened before the story begins.
- give information about the person in the story.

Example:

A Ferry Ride to Kowloon

A ferry ride to Kowloon changed my life forever. In June 1998, I was in Hong Kong with my friend Chen. On the last day of the trip, we planned to go sightseeing in Kowloon, but in the morning, Chen felt sick. He wanted to stay in the hotel, so I decided to go by myself.

This story is about how the writer met his wife. The first body sentences give background information about

- when and where the story happened: 1998 in Hong Kong.
- events that happened before the story begins: The writer planned to go on the trip with his friend, but his friend got sick and stayed at the hotel.

Focused Practice

A. *Read the beginning of the paragraphs. Which type of background information is in the paragraphs? Check (✓) one or more types of information. Then underline the information in the paragraph.*

Paragraph 1

An unexpected meeting with a teacher was the turning point in Hilda Solis's life. Hilda's family was poor. Her parents worked in a factory, and she had seven brothers and sisters. In high school, Hilda had little hope for her future. College was expensive, so she planned to work as a secretary in an office.

_____ **a.** When and where the story happened

___✓___ **b.** Events that happened before the story begins

___✓___ **c.** Information about the person in the story

Paragraph 2

> My father lost his job, but he found a new career and a new life. For 15 years, my father worked as a furniture salesperson. Then he lost his job because his company had financial problems and had to close. My father looked for a new job, but he did not find one.

_____ **a.** When and where the story happened

✓ **b.** Events that happened before the story begins

_____ **c.** Information about the people in the story

Paragraph 3

> Taking a filmmaking class was a turning point in my life. In my last year in high school, I had time for an extra class. There were only two classes available: French and filmmaking. I spoke French already, so I took the filmmaking class. I did not know anything about making films.

✓ **a.** When and where the story happened

✓ **b.** Events that happened before the story begins

_____ **c.** Information about the people in the story

B. *Compare your answers with a partner. Did you check (✓) the same information?*

Your Own Writing

Planning Your Body Sentences

A. *Look at your timeline on page 57, topic sentence on page 61, and notes on page 61. Think about your story.*

- What story do you want to tell?

- What are the events in the story?

- When did they happen?

- In what order did they happen?

Write your topic sentence. List the information you need to tell your story.

Topic Sentence: _____

_____

_____

_____

_____

_____

B. **Checking in.** *Share your information with a partner. Discuss these questions.*

1. Does the topic sentence introduce the story?

2. What is the turning point or memorable event?

3. Which information tells the events in the story?

4. Which information is background?

5. Which information is the most interesting?

6. Do you need to add more information to make anything clearer?

After your discussion, write five or more body sentences. Use time words to order the events in the story.

_____

_____

_____

_____

_____

_____

■ THE CONCLUDING SENTENCE

The concluding sentence is the last sentence in the paragraph. It tells the reader that the paragraph is ending. In Units 1 and 2, you learned that the concluding sentence often repeats or restates words or ideas from the topic sentence.

The concluding sentence can also add a final thought to the paragraph. A final thought is a comment about the experience.

The Basic Paragraph

▶ Topic Sentence
▶ Body Sentences
▼ Concluding Sentence
  • Repeat and Restate Words
  • Final Thought

Example:

A Ferry Ride to Kowloon

A ferry ride to Kowloon changed my life forever. In June 1998, I was in Hong Kong with my friend Chen. On the last day of the trip, we planned to go sightseeing in Kowloon, but in the morning, Chen felt sick. He wanted to stay in the hotel, so I decided to go by myself. I went to the ferry terminal and got my ticket. It was a sunny day, so I sat on the top deck of the ferry. Then a young woman sat next to me, and we started talking. Her name was Jing. She was on her way to work at a Kowloon hotel. After the one-hour trip, we felt like best friends. We emailed each other for months afterwards. The next summer, I visited her again. Now, she is my wife. I'm lucky that I did not miss the ferry that day.

Topic Sentence: A ferry ride to Kowloon changed my life forever.

Concluding Sentence: I'm lucky that I did not miss the ferry that day.

The concluding sentence repeats the word *ferry* and restates the idea *ferry ride→did not miss the ferry.*

It also makes a comment: *I'm lucky.*

Focused Practice

A. *Read the topic sentences and concluding sentences. Write the repeated or restated words. Then write the final thought.*

Example:

Topic Sentence: An unexpected meeting with a teacher changed Hilda Solis's life.

Concluding Sentence: Without Mr. Sanchez, Hilda's life might be very different.

Repeated or Restated Words: *a teacher, Mr. Sanchez*

Final Thought: *Hilda's life might be very different.*

1. **Topic Sentence:** My father's life changed when he lost his job as a furniture salesperson.

   Concluding Sentence: In the end, my father is happier today with his new career and his new life.

   Repeated or Restated Words:

   My father _____

   life _____

   job _____

   Final Thought: _____

2. **Topic Sentence:** Justin Bieber put his videos on YouTube, and his life was never the same.

   Concluding Sentence: After that, Justin Bieber became an international pop star.

   Repeated or Restated Words:

   Justin Bieber _____

   Final Thought: _____

3. **Topic Sentence:** The best day of my life was the day my soccer team won a championship.

   Concluding Sentence: On that day, I was a hero for my soccer team and my town.

   Repeated or Restated Words:

   my soccer team _____

   the best day _____

   Final Thought: _____

4. **Topic Sentence:** Running the Boston Marathon was an exciting day for my sister-in-law.

   Concluding Sentence: That day, Denise was very tired, but also very proud that she finished.

   Repeated or Restated Words:

   an exciting day _____

   my sister-in-law _____

   Final Thought: _____

5. **Topic Sentence:** I took a trip to Europe by myself and came home a different person.

   Concluding Sentence: My adventure in Europe taught me to be independent and self-confident.

   Repeated or Restated Words:

   I took a trip to Europe _____

   Final Thought: _____

B. *Read the paragraph. Work with a partner. Write a concluding sentence with a final thought.*

The Hoxne Hoard

A British farmer lost a hammer, and it changed his life. In 1992 in the town of Hoxne, England, a farmer lost his hammer in a field. He asked a friend to help him search for it. They did not find the hammer. Instead, they found a very old silver spoon, gold jewelry, and gold and silver coins. They called the police right away. The next day, archeologists[1] began to dig out the treasure. There were 14,865 gold, silver, and bronze coins. There was also tableware and jewelry. The treasure was more than 1,600 years old! A year later, the British government paid the farmer and his friend £1.75 million ($2.8 million). Today, you can see the "Hoxne Hoard" in the British Museum in London. _____

_____

_____

[1]**archeologist:** a person who studies ancient societies

Tip for Writers

Concluding Connectors. In a final thought, you can connect your concluding sentence to the paragraph by repeating or restating words and ideas from the topic sentence.

You can also use phrases to refer back to the story. Use a comma after the phrase if it begins the sentence. Here are some examples.

- *after that*
- *that day*
- *in the end*

Concluding Sentence: *I'm lucky that I did not miss the ferry **that day**.*

Concluding Sentence: ***After that,** I was able to follow my dreams.*

Underline the phrase that refers back to the story.

1. After that, I tried to drive more carefully.

2. In the end, my father is happier today with his new career.

3. That day, I was a hero for my soccer team and my town.

4. Justin Bieber became an international star after that.

5. My European adventure taught me to be independent in the end.

Your Own Writing

Planning Your Concluding Sentence

A. *Read your topic sentence and body sentences on page 69. Then answer the questions.*

1. Which words or ideas in the topic sentence do you want to repeat or restate in your concluding sentence? Write the words or ideas.

_____

_____

2. What final thoughts do you want to add? Write two final thoughts.

_____

_____

B. *Write a concluding sentence. Use the ideas above to help you.*

_____

_____

C. **Checking in.** *Share your topic sentence and concluding sentence with a partner. Did your partner . . .*

- restate ideas from the topic sentence in a different way?

- add a final thought?

- write an interesting concluding sentence for the story?

After your discussion, do you want to rewrite your concluding sentence? Make changes to the sentence, if necessary.

Writing Your First Draft

Write the first draft of your paragraph. Put your topic sentence, body sentences, and concluding sentence together in a paragraph. Give your paragraph a title. Hand in your first draft to your teacher.

Revising your draft is another important step. Revising is the time to make sure your paragraph has all the important information. When you revise, you make your writing clearer. You may need to change, add, or delete words or sentences, or move sentences to a different place in the paragraph.

Focused Practice

A. *Read the narrative paragraph.*

A Chance to Follow My Dreams

A college scholarship changed my life forever. I was a good student in high school, and I wanted to go to college. I wanted to become a doctor. This was also my parents' dream, but we did not have enough money for college tuition. I did not know what to do. Then a guidance counselor at school told me about a scholarship. The scholarship pays for college for me. I decided to apply. I worked on the application for several weeks. I had to write essays and answer a lot of questions. Finally, I mailed in the application. I waited a long time for the reply. Then one day, I got an envelope in the mail. I was afraid to open it. I knew the envelope contained my future. I gave it to my mother to open. She opened it and looked at the letter. Immediately, she smiled, and I knew it was good news. I got the scholarship, and after that, I was able to follow my dreams.

B. *Work with a partner. Answer the questions about the paragraph.*

1. What is the topic of the paragraph? Circle it.

2. What is the controlling idea of the paragraph? Underline it.

3. How many sentences talk about background information? _____

4. What time order words does the writer include? Put a star (*) next to them.

5. What is the concluding sentence? Underline it.

6. What is the final thought in the concluding sentence? Underline it a second time.

Your Own Writing

Revising Your Draft

A. *Reread the first draft of your paragraph. Use the Revision Checklist. What do you need to revise?*

B. *Revise your paragraph.*

Revision Checklist

Did you . . .

☐ tell the story of a turning point or memorable event that changed someone's life?

☐ include a topic sentence with a controlling idea?

☐ support the controlling idea with the body sentences?

☐ give background information that the reader needs to know?

☐ put body sentences in time order?

☐ include a concluding sentence that gives a final thought?

☐ use *and*, *but*, and *so* to join sentences?

Step 4   Editing

■ GRAMMAR PRESENTATION

Before you hand in your paragraph, read it again and look for errors in grammar. In this section you will review simple past regular and irregular verbs. Think about your paragraph as you review.

The Simple Past: Statements with Regular and Irregular Verbs

Grammar Notes	Examples
1. Use the **simple past** to tell about **things that are finished.** 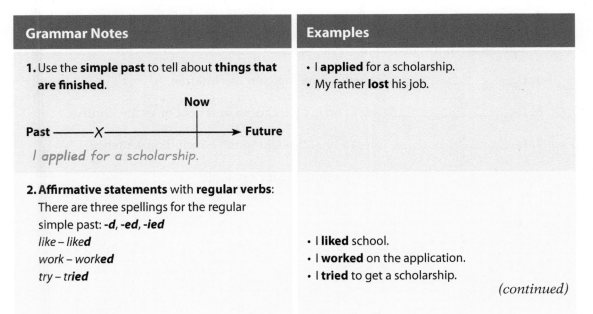	• I **applied** for a scholarship. • My father **lost** his job.
2. **Affirmative statements** with **regular verbs:** There are three spellings for the regular simple past: *-d*, *-ed*, *-ied* *like – liked* *work – worked* *try – tried*	• I **liked** school. • I **worked** on the application. • I **tried** to get a scholarship. *(continued)*

3. Affirmative statements with **irregular verbs**:
Irregular verbs do not add *-ed*. They often look different than the base form.
- *give – **gave***
- *have – **had***
- *find – **found***

- They **gave** me a scholarship.
- I **had** an important test.
- Carlos **found** a job.

4. The simple past verb form is the **same for all subject pronouns**.

- He **liked** school.
- We **worked** on the application.
- They **had** an important test.

5. Negative statements: Use *did not* + the base form of the verb.

BE CAREFUL: Do not use the simple past form after *did not*.

- I **did not have** money for school.
- Tara **did not know** her brother.

NOT: Tara ~~did not knew~~ her brother.

6. The past tense of *be* is *was* or *were*.

The **negative** of *was* is *was not*, and the negative of *were* is *were not*.

- Junko **was** a high school student.
- Her teachers **were** helpful.
- I **was not** good at math.
- The exams **were not** easy.

Focused Practice

A. *Which sentences are true for you? Complete the sentences with the simple past of the verb given. Use* **not** *for sentences that are not true for you.*

1. I _____ (choose) Assignment 1: A turning point in someone's life.

2. I _____ (pick) Assignment 2: A memorable event in someone's life.

3. I _____ (write) about a happy event—like finding a job or

   getting married.

4. I _____ (tell) the story of a difficult or challenging event—like losing

   a job or having an accident.

5. I _____ (research) my topic on the Internet.

6. I _____ (work) on my paragraph at school or in the library.

7. I _____ (give) a final thought in my concluding sentence.

8. I _____ (draw) a timeline for my topic.

B. *Read the paragraph. Correct seven more simple past errors.*

The Ugly Yellow Truck

                     took

  Renting an ugly yellow truck saved my life. Two years ago, I ~~take~~ a ski vacation in the Pyrenees Mountains. To get there, I have to rent a truck. It was big and yellow, and very ugly. I stayed at a mountain house for two days. I played in the snow and skied. Then, on the last night, there was an avalanche. It covered the house in snow. Some of the windows broke, and snow come into the house. The front door did not opened. I tryed to push it open, again and again, but it did not open. It gets colder and colder. By morning, I did not feel my fingers or toes. I did not knew what to do. Just then, I heard a sound from above—it was a helicopter! The pilot seed my yellow truck and came to save me. Before that trip, I hated the color yellow, but now it is my favorite color!

C. *Write three sentences for your assignment. Use the simple past in your sentences. They can be sentences you already have in your paragraph, or they can be new sentences.*

1. _____

2. _____

3. _____

Your Own Writing

Editing Your Draft

A. *Edit your paragraph for the assignment. Use the Editing Checklist below.*

B. *Write a clean copy of your paragraph. Give it to your teacher.*

Editing Checklist

Did you . . .

☐ use the past simple correctly?

☐ give your paragraph a title?

☐ format the paragraph correctly?

☐ use correct punctuation and capitalization?

☐ use new vocabulary words from this unit correctly?

Too Much Information

IN THIS UNIT You will write a persuasive paragraph about sharing information on the Internet.

These days, people put their name, address, photos, opinions, experiences, and much more on the Internet. It can help some people to find new friends, get better jobs, or even become famous. For other people, sharing personal information online creates a lot of problems. Some people feel that we share "too much information"—TMI. Do you share personal information on the Internet? How much information is TMI?

Planning for Writing

■ BRAINSTORM

A. *Read the webpage from a social networking site. Is any information TMI? Discuss with a partner.*

 Edgar Salazar I'm so bored at work today. I can't wait to go home!
Sanjay Singh Want to meet up? Call me. My number is 555-207-3482.

 Vicky Chen Support the rights of workers. Don't buy products from Magnicorp. Send this message to friends if you agree.

 Joey Trainor is in a relationship[1] with **Sarah Bayley**.

 Julie Jones Happy Birthday, Mom! I love you. You're the best!

 Junichiro Matsumoto Check out[2] these pictures of my trip to Hawaii!
Julie Jones Great pix![3] Looks like fun!
Ken Tange Jun, where did you get that ugly swim suit?! LOL![4]

[1] **in a relationship:** boyfriend or girlfriend with someone
[2] **check out:** (slang) look at
[3] **pix:** an abbreviation of "pictures," often used on the Internet
[4] **LOL:** an abbreviation of "laughing out loud," used on the Internet to say that something is funny

B. Using a T-Chart. A T-chart shows the pros (good things) and cons (bad things) of a topic. When you write an opinion, a T-chart can help you get ideas.

Write the pros and cons of online information sharing in the T-chart. Discuss your answers with a partner. Match the pros and cons with examples from Exercise A.

Sharing information online can . . .	
hurt someone's feelings	make someone laugh
✓ help you communicate with friends	make someone feel good
cause trouble at work or school	give personal information to people you do not know

Pros	Cons
	hurt someone's feelings

Don't Just Surf the Web—Be the Web!

1 You may get your news online. You may love online shopping. You may begin every vacation with the click of a mouse.[1] But if you are not putting *yourself* online, you are behind the times.[2]

2 To succeed in this modern world, you need an online presence.[3] An online presence is easy to create. You do not need to know very much about computers, and you do not need much time or money. With the following five types of websites, you can be part of the World Wide Web.

Social Networking Sites

3 Do you want to make new friends? Do you want to learn about your old friends? Join a social networking[4] website. On these sites, you can talk with friends, plan parties and events, and describe your personal interests. You might even find someone special from your past, for example, that cute classmate from high school.

Professional Networking Sites

4 If you are not interested in social networking, that's OK—the Web has a serious side too. Professional[5] networking sites are for working people. On these sites, you can talk with other professionals and get the latest information about your type of work. You can also find jobs. Many companies use professional networking sites to find new workers. Some people find jobs just 24 hours after joining a professional networking site. Who knows—maybe you will be next!

5 If you already have enough friends, and a job you like, the following sites can help you share your creative side.

File Sharing Sites

6 Do you sing, play piano, paint, draw, take pictures, or make movies? On file sharing sites, you can share your artwork and post[6] your favorite photographs or videos. These sites are free, and they just might make you famous! For example, a young girl named Michelle Phan posted videos on a file sharing site about beauty secrets. The videos became very popular. As a result, Michelle became the spokesperson for a large cosmetics company.

Personal Websites and Blogs

7 You may not be an artist, but you still have a personality you can share. On personal websites, you create your very own web page. There, you can post personal information, journals, and anything else. You can even make some money! For example, some websites will pay you to write about your favorite businesses.

Forums

8 Maybe you have an unusual hobby. Maybe you hate something most people like. On forum sites, you can talk with people who share your interests and opinions. There are forums for even the most unusual topics. Do you have a fear of butterflies? Then go to ihatebutterflies.com and find others like you. Remember, on the World Wide Web, you are never alone!

9 The Internet is a big, wonderful place—but do not just look at it! Try the five types of sites above and become a part of the Web.

---

[1] **with the click of a mouse:** using a small object that you connect to a computer to give the computer instructions
[2] **behind the times:** not doing things the modern way
[3] **online presence:** the information about you on the Internet
[4] **social networking:** connecting with old and new friends
[5] **professional:** related to a job or work
[6] **post:** to put a message or computer document on the Internet so everyone can see it

Building Word Knowledge

Internet Vocabulary. There is special vocabulary for the Internet. Some words only describe things on the Internet. Other words describe the Internet, but also have different meanings in the real world. Some Internet words are both nouns and verbs. When you look up Internet words in the dictionary, be sure to look for the correct form and meaning to talk about the Internet. Here are some examples of Internet vocabulary.

- *My cousin has a **blog**. She **blogs** about local restaurants.*
- *This website has free music **downloads**. I **downloaded** three songs onto my computer.*
- *People share different types of **files** on the Internet, such as videos, music, and pictures.*
- *She **posted** a comment about her boss on the Internet. Her boss saw the **post**.*
- *I took pictures at the party, and then **uploaded** them to a website.*
- *My computer got a **virus**; now it doesn't work very well.*

A. *Use your dictionary. Write the "Internet" definition of the words.*

1. a blog _____

2. download _____

3. a file _____

4. post _____

5. upload _____

6. a virus _____

B. *Look at the example sentences in Building Word Knowledge above. Underline the nouns. Circle the verbs.*

C. *Complete the sentences. Use the correct form of one of the words above.*

1. I have to take my computer to the repair shop because it has a _____.

It doesn't work now.

2. When you get a new computer, you have to transfer all the _____ from

your old computer, including photos and music.

3. After each class, my teacher _____ messages about our homework on

the school's website.

4. My Internet connection is really slow; it takes a long time to _____

files onto my computer.

(continued)

5. I used to keep a journal, but now I write a _____ online instead. Many

people read it every week.

6. After I take pictures, I _____ the photographs from my camera to a

photo sharing website.

Focused Practice

A. *Read the website on page 80 again. Check (✓) the main idea of the reading.*

_____ **a.** In the modern world, there are many different types of websites.

_____ **b.** People need an online presence for success in today's world.

_____ **c.** To be successful in today's world, people must go online for news and
    shopping.

_____ **d.** In the modern world, file sharing sites can help you become famous.

B. *Make inferences. Which type of website should each person visit? Match the person with a website. Write the number.*

1. Hassan loves old cars. He wants to talk about his favorite types of old cars with other people.

2. Kendra is a teacher. She teaches math. She wants to talk with other math teachers.

3. Xiaoyan is a singer. She records her songs. She wants other people to enjoy her music.

4. Martin just moved back to his hometown. He wants to connect with his high school friends.

5. Belinda writes about environmental problems in her country. She wants to share her writing.

6. Hector is planning a vacation to Honduras. He wants to talk with other people about Honduras.

_____ **a.** Social networking sites

_____ **b.** Professional networking sites

_____ **c.** File sharing

_____ **d.** Personal website / blog

_____ **e.** Forum

C. *Discuss your answers with a small group.*

1. Does the author of the reading on page 80 think the Internet is a safe place? Explain.

2. Does the author think most people hate butterflies? Explain.

3. Which of the types of websites in the reading do you use? Why do you use them?

4. Which of the types of websites in the reading do you not use? Why not?

5. In your group, who has the biggest online presence? Explain.

Tip for Writers

Thinking about Audience. In Unit 1, you learned about writing for an audience. Your audience is the person who will read your writing.

When you persuade someone, you try to make someone agree with you. When you write a persuasive paragraph, it is helpful to think of a *specific* audience for your writing. Then you can choose reasons for your opinion and examples for your specific audience. This will make your writing more persuasive for your reader. Here are some examples.

- In your opinion, people should use social networking sites.

  Before you write, think of a friend or relative who does not use them a lot.

OR

- In your opinion, people should *not* use social network sites.

  Before you write, think of someone who uses them a lot.

Then ask yourself these questions:

What do you know about that person?

How can you persuade that person to change his or her mind?

A. *Think of a type of website, for example, a social networking site, a personal website, or blog. Then think of a person you know who does not use the website, such as a friend, classmate, or grandparent. Write the type of website and the person below.*

Type of Website: _____

Person: _____

B. *Work with a partner. How can you persuade the person in Exercise A to use the website? Discuss the questions.*

1. What do you know about the person? Why does this person *not* use the website?

2. Why do you think the person should use the website? Why do you think the person will like it?

3. What can you say to persuade the person to use it?

C. *Write three sentences to the person in Exercise A. Write three reasons why you think the person will like the website.*

1. _____

2. _____

3. _____

Writing a Persuasive Paragraph

In this unit you are going to write a persuasive paragraph. A persuasive paragraph tries to make the reader agree with an opinion. In your persuasive paragraph, you will write about sharing personal information on the Internet. Like other paragraphs, a persuasive paragraph has a topic sentence with a controlling idea, body sentences about the topic, and a concluding sentence.

The Persuasive Paragraph

▶ Topic Sentence
▶ Body Sentences
▶ Concluding Sentence

Step 1   Prewriting

Prewriting is an important step in the writing process. It helps you choose your topic and get ideas for your paragraph. In this prewriting, after you choose your topic, you brainstorm ideas about the topic: What do you already know about it? What do you want to learn about it? You write the pros and cons in a T-chart. These notes and the chart can help you write your paragraph.

Your Own Writing

Choosing Your Assignment

A. *Choose Assignment 1 or Assignment 2.*

Assignment 1: Write a persuasive paragraph about sharing information on the Internet and answer one of these questions:

• Why should people share certain types of information on the Internet?

• Why should people use certain types of websites?

Assignment 2: Write a persuasive paragraph about not sharing information on the Internet and answer one of these questions:

• Why should people *not* share certain types of information on the Internet?

• Why should people *not* use certain types of websites?

B. *Check (✓) the websites people should use and the information people should share. Put an X next to the type of websites and information people should **not** use or share.*

Websites

_____ Social networking sites

_____ Professional networking sites

_____ File sharing sites

_____ Personal web pages or blogs

_____ Forums

Types of Information

_____ Address or phone number

_____ Opinions about politics or social issues

_____ Opinions about other people

_____ Opinions about work or school

_____ Relationship status (single, married, dating)

_____ Photos from vacation

_____ Photos from school or work

_____ Funny videos

You own ideas: _____

➡

C. Freewriting is a kind of thinking on paper. In freewriting, it is important to continue writing without stopping. You do not worry about whether your ideas are good or bad. You do not worry about spelling or grammar. You just write and keep writing until you have new ideas. If you do not have any ideas, you can write, "I don't have any ideas." You do not stop thinking if you have no ideas. You keep thinking until an idea comes into your mind.

Choose a website or type of information for your assignment. Freewrite for five minutes about the topic. Here are some questions to get you started:

- What do you know about the website or type of information you chose?
- Do you think the website or information sharing is useful? Why or why not?
- What are the pros of the website or type of information? What are the cons?
- Do you think people share too much information online? Why or why not?
- Do your friends and relatives agree with you about sharing information online? Why or why not?

D. Checking in. *Share your ideas with a partner. Ask your partner questions and find out about your partner's opinion. For example:*

- What is the website or type of information?
- What are the pros and cons?
- What is your opinion? Why do you have this opinion?

After your discussion, add new ideas to your freewriting, if helpful.

E. *Complete the T-chart for your assignment. Write the topic: the type of website or information you are going to write about. Then write the pros and cons of your topic.*

Topic:	
Pros	**Cons**

■ THE TOPIC SENTENCE

The topic sentence of a paragraph includes the topic and controlling idea of the paragraph. In a persuasive paragraph, the controlling idea is the writer's opinion about the topic. For this assignment, the topic is a type of website or online sharing. The controlling idea is your personal opinion about it.

The Persuasive Paragraph

▼ Topic Sentence
- Topic and Controlling Idea
  - Your Opinion

▶ Body Sentences
▶ Concluding Sentence

Examples:

Topic Sentence: Social networking sites can be harmful.

The **topic** is: social networking sites

The **controlling idea** is the writer's opinion about the topic: They can be harmful (for everyone).

You can also make the topic sentence more specific. It can be about a specific group or person.

Topic Sentence: Social networking sites can be harmful **for students**.

Tip for Writers

Opinions and Facts. It is important to know the difference between opinions and facts. In a persuasive paragraph, the controlling idea is your opinion. You can support your opinion with facts. Facts can make your opinion more persuasive.

An **opinion** is an idea that people may disagree about. In writing, an opinion often begins with *I think that, I believe that,* or *In my opinion.* Here are some examples.

- *I think that video file sharing sites are easy to use.*
- *I believe that posting personal videos online is dangerous.*
- *In my opinion, professional networking sites are very helpful.*

A **fact** is true information. You can prove or measure facts. People do not usually disagree about a fact. Here are some examples.

- *YouTube and Vimeo are video sharing websites.*
- *YouTube started in February 2005.*
- *Vimeo had 3 million users in 2011.*

Read the pairs of sentences. Is the sentence Fact (F) or Opinion (O)? Write F *or* O.

1. _____ **a.** You can ask and answer questions on the website Formspring.

   _____ **b.** I believe that everyone should use Formspring to ask and answer questions.

2. _____ **a.** A blog is an easy way to create an online presence.

   _____ **b.** A blog is an online journal.

3. _____ **a.** Professional networking sites are not very useful.

_____ **b.** Professional networking sites are for working people.

4. _____ **a.** LinkedIn can help people quickly find a job anywhere.

_____ **b.** LinkedIn has users in over 200 countries around the world.

5. _____ **a.** There are several music sharing websites on the Internet.

_____ **b.** In my opinion, music sharing websites are useful for music lovers.

Focused Practice

A. _Circle the topic of each sentence. Underline the controlling idea. Does the topic sentence focus on a specific group? Put a star (*) next to the group._

Example:

(Social networking sites) can be harmful for *students.

1. Posting a résumé online is useful for job seekers.

2. In my opinion, a lot of personal information online can hurt a person's career.

3. Social networking sites help families stay close and connected.

4. I believe that social networking sites are not useful for businesses.

5. Internet forums are a good way to share opinions.

B. _Read the paragraph. Circle and write the best topic sentence for the paragraph._

Online Shopping

_____

_____

The main reason is that you can find anything you need online. For example, I like one kind of makeup, but the stores near my house do not sell it. I have to go to the mall across town. However, I can order it online with no problem. The other reason is that you can get better prices online. The makeup is usually more expensive in the store. A lot of online stores sell it, so I can look for the cheapest price. For these reasons, you should try shopping online.

---

a. Online shopping is difficult for most people.

b. There are many online shopping sites.

c. Online shopping sites are convenient for shoppers.

C. *Choose one idea from each box and complete the topic sentences. Write your own opinion. Compare your sentences with a partner. Do you agree or disagree with your partner's opinion?*

Box 1	Box 2	Box 3
photo sharing websites	dangerous	busy people
social networking sites	fun	students
posting personal photos	harmful	businesspeople
online shopping sites	interesting	children
posting political opinions	useful	students

1. _____ can be _____ for
   Box 1   Box 2

   _____.
   Box 3

2. _____ can be _____ for
   Box 1   Box 2

   _____.
   Box 3

Your Own Writing

Finding Out More

A. *Go online. Type the keywords* music sharing, photo sharing, video sharing, discussion forum, social networking, *or* blog, *or type the name of a specific website. Look at the main page of the website. Try to answer these questions:*

1. Who uses the site? For example, is it for professionals, adults, children, or artists?

   _____

2. What do people do on the website? For example, can you create a blog, share your photos, or connect with friends?

   _____

3. What does the website look like? Are there pictures or just writing? Is the page crowded or simple?

   _____

4. Does the website give any numbers? For example, does it give the number of users, number of posts, or number of files?

   _____

5. Can people post information on the website? What kind of information or messages can people post on the website?

_____

6. What kind of files can you upload or download?

_____

7. Are there words such as *About, FAQ, Explore,* or *What's New*? Click on the words. What information is there?

_____

B. Checking in. *Share your information with a partner. Did your partner find out . . .*

• what people do on the website?

• the number of people, posts, or files on the website?

• the kind of messages and information you can post on the website?

After your discussion, add new ideas to your information, if helpful.

Planning Your Topic Sentence

A. *Think about the assignment. What is your topic: a type of information sharing or a type of website? Write your topic.*

Topic: _____

B. *Write words that give your opinion about your topic. Use ideas from the box or add your own ideas.*

Positive words	Negative words
useful	problems
helpful	harmful
fun	dangerous
interesting	a waste of time[1]
a good way to share	a bad way to share

[1] **a waste of time:** a bad use of someone's time

Opinion Words: _____

C. *Write a topic sentence. Use your T-chart, your freewriting, and your notes above to help you. Remember: You can begin with* In my opinion, I believe that, *or* I think that.

Topic Sentence: _____

_____

■ THE BODY SENTENCES

The body sentences form the largest part of a paragraph. In the body of a paragraph, you develop and support the controlling idea in your topic sentence. Remember: All the body sentences are about the one topic and the controlling idea.

In a persuasive paragraph, the body sentences should include:

- two or three reasons for your opinion. The reasons explain why you have your opinion, and they make the reader think about your opinion.

- one or two details, facts, or examples to explain each reason. These help the reader understand your reasons.

A paragraph with good reasons and clear explanations helps the reader understand your opinion. It can persuade the reader that your opinion is correct.

The Persuasive Paragraph

▶ Topic Sentence

▼ Body Sentences

  • Development and Support
    • Giving Reasons
    • Expanding Your Reasons

▶ Concluding Sentence

Example:

Social Networking Sites

I think that social networking sites are harmful for students. The first reason is that the sites are a waste of time. For example, my roommate is online all the time. He opens his book to study, but then he chats with friends on the Internet instead. He does not finish his homework because he is always chatting on social networking websites. The second reason is that many students share too much information online. For instance, they post pictures of parties and write personal notes to their boyfriend or girlfriend. They tell everyone their personal information. This information can change people's opinion of them.

Topic: Social Networking Sites

Controlling Idea (the writer's opinion): They are harmful for students.

Reason 1: *The sites are a waste of time.*

Example: *My roommate is online all the time.*

Reason 2: *Many students share too much information online.*

Example: *They post pictures of parties, write personal notes, and tell personal information.*

Building Word Knowledge

Transition Words. To make your opinion clear and persuasive, use transitions to introduce each reason. Here are some examples.

Transitions for Reason 1	Transitions for Reason 2	Transitions for Reason 3
The first reason is that	*The second reason is that*	*The third reason is that*
The main reason is that	*Another reason is that*	*Another reason is that*
First of all,	*Secondly,*	*The final reason is that*
First,	*In addition,*	*Lastly,*

A. *Read the sentences. Number the sentences in the correct order to form a paragraph. Then write the paragraph on a separate piece of paper.*

My Blog

_____ **a.** Secondly, my blog lets me share my ideas and feelings.

_____ **b.** First, my blog is a good way to practice my English.

_____ **c.** For these reasons, my blog is very helpful to me.

_____ **d.** For example, I can learn new vocabulary and practice my writing.

_____ **e.** For instance, I often feel confused in this new country, and I write about this in my blog.

__1__ **f.** I believe that blogs are helpful for learning English.

B. *Complete the paragraph. Use transitions to introduce each reason.*

Laptop Computers

I think people should not use laptop computers. _____

_____ laptops sometimes break. For example, I spilled coffee on my laptop

one time, and it stopped working. _____ you

can lose a laptop. People often forget laptops on the train, at the library, or in a

café. _____ people often steal laptops. For

instance, I read a report about a computer theft survey. According to the survey,

there were over 5,500,000 computers stolen in the United States between 2007

and 2010.

Focused Practice

A. *Read the paragraph. Answer the questions with a partner.*

Family Recipes

Recipe websites are fun for people who love to cook. The first reason is that you can share the recipes with your family. For example, my grandmother makes a delicious dessert from the north of Peru. All my cousins love it, but we did not have the recipe. We live in different cities and countries. My aunt posted the recipe on the Internet, and now all my cousins have it. Another reason is that you can share the recipes with other food lovers. Many people around the world love to cook. They want to learn new recipes. After my aunt posted the recipe, she got email messages from people in Spain, the United States, and even Japan. People tried the recipe and loved it. For these reasons, if you like to cook, you should share your recipes online.

---

1. What is the topic sentence?

2. What is the topic?

3. What is the controlling idea (the writer's opinion)?

4. How many reasons does the writer give for this opinion?

5. How many examples are there?

6. Do you agree with the author after reading this paragraph?

B. *Match the reasons and the topic sentences. Discuss your answers with a partner.*

Topic Sentence 1:

I think that posting photos online is a bad idea.

Reasons: __b__, _____, _____

Topic Sentence 2:

In my opinion, posting photos online is fun.

Reasons: _____, _____, _____

a. I like to see my friends' comments about my pictures.

b. I do not want everyone to see pictures of private events, such as family vacations.

c. Strangers will know too much about my private life.

d. I can see the places my friends visit on vacation.

e. I can show my friends pictures of my children.

f. My friend Pyotr, a professional photographer, says that people steal his pictures online.

C. *Complete the paragraphs. Circle the best example.*

Paragraph 1

Online Photo Sharing

In my opinion, posting photos online is fun. The main reason is that I like to see my friends' comments about my pictures. For example, _____

---

a. I posted pictures from my birthday party. My friends posted a lot of funny comments about them.

b. my friend posted photos of his vacation to Hawaii. The photos were so beautiful. Now I want to go to Hawaii!

Paragraph 2

Internet Discussion Forums

I think that Internet discussion forums can be harmful. First of all, many comments on forums are not nice. For instance, _____

---

a. I am not a mean person. I like to say nice things to people on the Internet.

b. sometimes people say you are not intelligent, or a bad person, because you have a different opinion.

Paragraph 3

Travel Blogs

In my opinion, travel blogs are a good way to share your travel experiences. One reason is that you can keep a record of your travels. For example, _____

---

a. last year I wrote a travel blog about my trip around the United States. Now I can look at it and remember all the places that I visited.

b. last year I took at trip around the United States. I took my laptop with me and wrote a travel blog.

Your Own Writing

Planning Your Body Sentences

A. *Write your topic sentence from page 89. Write two reasons to support your opinion. Write examples to support your reasons. Use your T-Chart and your freewriting on page 85 and your notes on page 88 to help you.*

Topic Sentence: _____

_____

Reason 1: _____

_____

Examples: _____

_____

_____

_____

Reason 2: _____

_____

Examples: _____

_____

_____

_____

B. Checking in. *Share your sentences with a partner. Discuss these questions.*

1. What is your partner's opinion about the topic?

2. Do all the reasons and examples support the opinion?

3. Who is the audience? Do the reasons and examples explain the opinion clearly for that audience?

4. Does your partner need to add more information to make anything clearer? What can your partner add?

After your discussion, do you want to rewrite your body sentences? Make changes to the sentences, if necessary.

THE CONCLUDING SENTENCE

The concluding sentence is the last sentence in the paragraph. It tells the reader that the paragraph is ending. The concluding sentence often repeats or restates words or ideas from the topic sentence.

In a persuasive paragraph, the concluding sentence often gives advice to the reader. It says the reader *should* or *should not* do something. It can refer back to the reasons in the paragraph with transition words such as *clearly* or *for these reasons*.

> **The Persuasive Paragraph**
>
> ▶ Topic Sentence
> ▶ Body Sentences
> ▼ Concluding Sentence
>   • Giving Advice

Example:

Topic Sentence: I think that social networking sites are harmful for students.

Concluding Sentence: For these reasons, students should not use social networking sites very often.

The **controlling idea** is: social networking sites are harmful for students.

The **concluding advice** is: students should not use social networking sites very often.

The **transition words** are: *For these reasons*

Focused Practice

A. *Reread the paragraph "Family Recipes" on page 92. Copy the topic and concluding sentences below. Then answer the questions.*

Topic Sentence: _____

_____

Concluding Sentence: _____

_____

1. What is the controlling idea in the topic sentence?

_____

2. What words in the concluding sentence repeat words in the topic sentence?

_____

3. What words in the concluding sentence restate words in the topic sentence?

_____

4. What transition words are in the concluding sentence?

_____

B. *Read the sentences. Number the sentences in the correct order. Use the transition words to help. Then write the paragraph.*

Free Music Sharing Websites

_____ **a.** For example, my friend Kyung got a virus and lost all the files on his computer.

__1__ **b.** I think free music sharing websites are dangerous.

_____ **c.** First of all, your computer can get a virus from these sites.

_____ **d.** Clearly, free music sharing websites just are not safe.

_____ **e.** The second reason is that some free music sharing websites are illegal.

_____ **f.** Students often use these websites, but they do not know it is not legal.

_____

_____

_____

_____

_____

C. *Read the topic sentence. Circle the best concluding sentence.*

1. **Topic Sentence:** Social networking sites help families stay close and connected.

   a. For these reasons, people should not use social networking sites.

   b. For these reasons, everyone should try social networking.

2. **Topic Sentence:** I think Internet forums are not a good way to share political opinions.

   a. Clearly, people should share their ideas in person, not online.

   b. Clearly, people should use Internet forums to discuss politics.

3. **Topic Sentence:** I believe that online video sites are entertaining.

   a. People should look for interesting videos online.

   b. You should not waste time on video sharing sites.

4. **Topic Sentence:** File sharing sites are a great way to share my artwork with other artists.

   a. For these reasons, artists should be careful about posting their work online.

   b. For these reasons, artists should share their work online.

5. Topic Sentence: In my opinion, posting personal photos online can hurt your career.

    a. Clearly, everyone should share personal pictures online.

    b. Clearly, you should be careful about posting photos on the Web.

D. *Read the paragraph. Write a concluding sentence and give advice.*

Sharing Personal Information Online

T S

    I think sharing your personal information online is a bad idea. The first reason is that it is dangerous. For example, someone might learn your home address and that may not be safe. Secondly, strange people can call you. For instance, I put my phone number online. A man called me and asked for money. It made me really uncomfortable. In the end, I had to change my phone number. _____

_____

Your Own Writing

Planning Your Concluding Sentence

A. *Write your topic sentence from page 94. Write a concluding sentence that gives advice.*

Topic Sentence: _____

Concluding Sentence: _____

B. Checking in. *Share your topic sentence and concluding sentence with a partner. Discuss these questions.*

    1. Does the concluding sentence give advice?

    2. If yes, what is the advice?

    3. If no, what advice do you suggest?

After your discussion, do you want to rewrite your concluding sentence? Make changes to the sentence, if necessary.

Writing Your First Draft

Write the first draft of your paragraph. Put your topic sentence, body sentences, and concluding sentence together in a paragraph. Give your paragraph a title. Hand in your first draft to your teacher.

Step 3 Revising

Revising your work is an important part of the writing process. You can make sure that your paragraph has enough information and that the information supports the topic sentence.

Focused Practice

A. *Read the persuasive paragraph.*

Posting Class Assignments Online

I think that posting class assignments online is a good idea. First of all, students can check the dates of important exams and assignments easily. For instance, my math teacher has a web page. She uploads her class schedule there. We can check the date of our math exams on her web page. In addition, teachers can save paper. For example, my history teacher uses a lot of paper to print homework instructions. It is not necessary. He can post the homework instructions online and save hundreds of pieces of paper. Clearly, teachers should post their class assignments online.

B. *Work with a partner. Answer the questions about the paragraph.*

1. What is the topic of the paragraph? Circle it.
2. What is the controlling idea of the paragraph (the writer's opinion)? Underline it.
3. What reasons support the writer's opinion? Put a star (*) next to the reasons.
4. What examples explain the reasons? Put a check (✓) next to the examples.
5. What is the concluding sentence? Underline it.

Your Own Writing

Revising Your Draft

A. *Reread the first draft of your paragraph. Use the Revision Checklist. What do you need to revise?*

B. *Revise your paragraph.*

Revision Checklist

Did you . . .

☐ give an opinion about sharing information on the Internet?

☐ give reasons and examples for your opinion?

☐ restate your opinion and give advice in the concluding sentence?

Step 4 Editing

◼ GRAMMAR PRESENTATION

Before you hand in your revised paragraph, read it again and look for errors in grammar. In this section, you will review modal verbs. *Will, may, might, should,* and *can* are modal verbs. Think about your paragraph as you review these verbs.

Modal Verbs

Grammar Notes	Examples

1. Use the **base form** of the verb after **modal verbs**.	• I **may write** about Facebook.
	• You **should try** Facebook.
	  Not: You should ~~to try~~ Facebook.
	  You should ~~tries~~ Facebook.

2. Modal verbs have different meanings. • Use *will* to make **predictions** about the future. • Use *may* and *might* to talk about **possibilities** in the future. • Use *should* to give **advice**. • Use *can* to express **ability** or **possibility**.	• My roommate **will** go online tonight. • She **may** stay on for hours. • She **might** do a video chat. • She **should** study more often. • You **can** watch videos online.
3. *Won't* is the contraction of *will + not*. Use *won't* in speaking and informal writing.	• I **will not** go online tonight. • I **won't** join a professional networking site.
4. *Shouldn't* is the contraction of *should + not*. Use *shouldn't* in speaking and informal writing.	• You **should not** email strangers • You **shouldn't** share personal information online.
5. *Can't* and *cannot* are the contractions of *can + not*. Use *can't* in speaking and informal writing, and *cannot* in formal speaking and writing.	• I **can't** wait to go home. • Students **cannot** use the computer lab.
6. Do not use contractions for *may + not* or *might + not*.	• In 10 years, we **may not** use email anymore. • We **might not** use computers.

Focused Practice

A. *Read the sentences. Circle the modal verbs.*

1. Hector might start his own blog.

2. Children should not surf the Web alone.

3. My grandfather won't try online file sharing.

4. How can I persuade you to try social networking?

5. Abdur's computer has a virus, so he may get a new one.

6. I like Internet forums because I can talk about my favorite hobbies.

B. *Complete the sentences. Circle the best modal verb.*

1. In my opinion, you (**may not / should not / will not**) use social networking sites.

2. You (**might not / can't / won't**) visit that website right now. It isn't working.

3. I'm not sure, but I (**may / will / should**) work on my blog tonight.

4. I'm sure that everyone (**should / might / will**) have a computer in the future.

5. You (**will / may / should**) try this new online game. It's really fun.

6. Mark does all his work on a computer. He (**can / may / should**) type really fast.

7. I don't look at social networking sites at work. My boss (**should / can / might**) see

me and get angry.

C. *Read the paragraph. Correct five more modal verb errors.*

The Advantages of Social Networking Sites

I think social networking sites help friends and family communicate. First, they
                                                                bother
are very convenient. A phone call can ~~to bother~~ people because they mays be

busy. For example, the phone call may interrupts their dinner. An online message

willn't bother people because they can answer the message anytime they want.

The second reason is that social networking sites are free. A telephone can costs

a lot. For example, my parents pay $50 a month for their telephone line. For these

reasons, I think people should used social networking sites to communicate.

D. *Write five sentences for your assignment. Use modals in your sentences. They can be sentences you already have in your paragraph, or they can be new sentences.*

1. _____

2. _____

3. _____

4. _____

5. _____

Your Own Writing

Editing Your Draft

A. *Edit your paragraph for the assignment. Use the Editing Checklist below.*

B. *Write a clean copy of your paragraph. Give it to your teacher.*

Editing Checklist

Did you . . .

☐ use the correct form of modal verbs?

☐ choose modals with the correct meaning?

☐ use transition words to introduce your reasons, examples, and conclusions?

☐ use new vocabulary words from this unit correctly?

☐ format the paragraph correctly?

☐ give your paragraph a title?

☐ use correct capitalization and punctuation?

5 Business Solutions

IN THIS UNIT   You will write a paragraph about a business with a problem, and give possible solutions.

Some businesses just do not get it right. They do not accept credit cards. They close too early. Their prices are too high. Their stores are dirty or not organized well. They are not polite to customers. These businesses have problems. They need to find solutions or they will lose customers. What other kinds of problems can a business have?

Planning for Writing

■ BRAINSTORM

A. *Read about Dina's business. What problem did it have? Was Dina's solution a good solution? Discuss your answer with a partner.*

═══════════════ FASHION TO GO ═══════════════

Two years ago, Dina's dream came true. The 27-year-old fashion designer opened her own store. She finally had a place to sell her creative clothing, but there was one problem—she had no customers. Dina tried many ways to get customers. First, she made a new sign. Then, she advertised online and in the newspaper, but nothing worked. Finally, she discovered the

problem. Her store was too far from downtown. People had to drive a long way to get to her store. In the end, Dina found an interesting solution to her problem. She closed the store and bought an old van. Now, she sells clothing from her van. She named her business "Fashion to Go." Each day, she drives to a different part of town. "I have customers all over the city," she laughs. Dina brought her clothes to her customers, and that is how she found success.

B. Using a Problem-Solution Chart. A problem-solution chart helps you think about problems and solutions. It helps you answer these questions: What is the problem? Why is it a problem? What are the solutions?

Read the article about Dina again. Work with a partner. Write the sentences in the problem-solution chart.

> She bought a van and sold her clothing in different places.
>
> She did not have any customers.
>
> The customers did not want to drive to the store.

Dina's Problem-Solution Chart

> **Problem**
> What was Dina's problem?
> _____

⬇

> **Reasons**
> Why did Dina have the problem?
> _____

⬇

> **Solutions**
> What was Dina's solution?
> _____

Domino's Strange Advertising: Our Pizza Tastes Bad

1   In 2007, Domino's Pizza was in trouble. Customers were not happy. Profits[1] were down by 55 percent.

2   Domino's studied the negative comments people made about them on the Internet. Most people did not like Domino's pizza. "It's boring," said one customer. Others did not like the flavor. "The sauce is like ketchup," said one person. "It tastes like the pizza box," another person said.

3   How could Domino's solve its problems? They had three ideas:

   (a) Pay a famous person to say the pizza tastes good.
   (b) Ask the company president to travel across the country and say the pizza tastes good.
   (c) Say the pizza tastes *bad*. Then promise to change it.

Surprisingly, Domino's chose option c.

4   In TV advertisements, Domino's employees[2] read the negative comments. They apologized for making bad pizza. Then they promised to make better pizza, with different cheese, different bread, and a new sauce.

5   The experts[3] did not think it was a good plan. They expected Domino's to lose more customers. But then something surprising happened. Sales went up immediately.

6   At first, Domino's thought customers were just curious about the new pizza flavor. They thought people would quickly lose interest. But sales stayed strong. By 2010, profits went up 55 percent.

7   What made Domino's "new pizza" a success? One expert explained, "Domino's said the product had problems, so the message was believable."

8   This was not the first promise that Domino's made to customers. In 1973, they promised to deliver[4] a pizza in 30 minutes. If not, the pizza was free. Domino's gave away a lot of pizzas, but they also got a lot of new customers. Soon, Domino's grew into an international company.

9   Today Domino's has over 9,000 stores in 60 countries. Clearly, other companies can learn from Domino's. In business, honesty is the most important ingredient.[5]

---

[1] **profit:** money that you gain by selling things or doing business, after you pay all other costs
[2] **employees:** people who are paid to work for someone else
[3] **expert:** someone who has special skill or knowledge of a subject
[4] **deliver:** to take food, packages, etc., to a particular place or person
[5] **ingredient:** a quality you need for success

Building Word Knowledge

Building Word Families. Many English words are part of a word family. When you learn a new word, it is helpful to learn other words in the same family. For example, many words have a related noun and verb form. Use a dictionary to help you find and use the correct word forms. Here are some examples.

Noun	Verb
expectation	expect
success	succeed
attraction	attract
increase	increase
improvement	improve

A. *Add the missing word forms. Use a dictionary to help you.*

Noun	Verb
1. _____	advertise
2. apology	_____
3. delivery	_____
4. explanation	_____
5. _____	promise
6. _____	sell
7. _____	suggest

B. *Complete the sentences. Write the correct word form.*

1. First Street Café does not _____ many customers.
   (attract / attraction)

2. The service at Lucky Garden Restaurant needs _____.
   (improve / improvement)

3. SuperShoes never gives an _____ for its mistakes.
   (apologize / apology)

4. The clothing store near my house is having a _____.
   (sale / sell)

5. Many restaurants _____ food to their customers.
   (deliver / delivery)

6. The customer service people can _____ the problem.
   (explain / explanation)

7. I have many good _____ for the company.
   (suggest / suggestions)

Focused Practice

A. *Read the article on page 104 again. Number the events in order. Write 1 for the first event and 6 for the last event.*

_____ **a.** Domino's listened to its customers.

_____ **b.** Today Domino's has stores in 60 countries.

___1___ **c.** Domino's sold fewer pizzas than before.

_____ **d.** Domino's profits went up by 55 percent.

_____ **e.** Domino's made a new advertisement.

B. *Complete the sentences. Circle the correct word.*

1. Customers did not like the _____ of Domino's pizza.

   a. price

   b. taste

   c. advertising

2. Domino's solution was unusual because they _____.

   a. said the pizza tasted bad

   b. made a TV commercial

   c. made pizza that tasted better

3. Experts say that Domino's solution was successful because _____.

   a. the pizza tasted great

   b. customers were curious

   c. Domino's was honest

4. Because of its new pizza, Domino's _____.

   a. opened 9,000 new stores

   b. increased profits by 55 percent

   c. gave away a lot of free pizza

5. Because of Domino's success, the company _____.

   a. opened stores all over the world

   b. lowered the price of pizza

   c. taught other companies about the pizza business

C. *Discuss your answers with a small group.*

1. Does the author have a positive opinion of Domino's? Explain.

2. What do you think of Domino's solution to their business problem? Was it a good idea?

3. Do you know about any other unusual solutions to business problems? What are they?

4. Are most companies honest like Domino's? Explain.

Writing a Problem-Solution Paragraph

In this unit, you are going to write a problem-solution paragraph. Like other paragraphs, the topic sentence of a problem-solution paragraph says the topic and controlling idea. The body of a problem-solution paragraph has two parts: The first part explains the problem, and the second part suggests a solution to the problem. The concluding sentence often restates the idea in the topic sentence or gives a final thought. The final thought is often a prediction, or guess about the future.

> **The Problem-Solution Paragraph**
>
> ▶ Topic Sentence
> ▶ Body Sentences
> ▶ Concluding Sentence

Step 1   Prewriting

Prewriting helps you think about ideas for your assignment. In this prewriting, you choose your assignment, and you write and discuss ideas about the problem and solution. Then you make a problem-solution chart to organize ideas for your writing.

Your Own Writing

Choosing Your Assignment

A. *Choose Assignment 1 or Assignment 2.*

   Assignment 1: Write about a large business—a company or corporation—with a problem. Describe the problem. Then suggest solutions.

   Assignment 2: Write about a small, local business with a problem. A local business is a business in your neighborhood or town. Describe the problem. Then suggest solutions.

B. *Make a list of companies or local businesses. Use the ideas below or your own ideas. Check (✔) the companies or businesses with problems. Then choose a company or business for your assignment.*

Companies and Corporations	**Local Businesses**
Restaurant chain: _____Domino's_____	Local restaurant: _____
Automobile company: _____	Clothing store: _____Fashion to Go_____
Computer company: _____	Bookstore: _____
Food company: _____	Grocery store: _____
Your own idea: _____	Your own idea: _____

C. *Freewrite for five minutes about your assignment topic. Write all ideas. Keep writing. Do not worry about good or bad ideas. Write any ideas you have about the topic. Here are some questions to get you started.*

   • What do you know about this business?

   • Why does this business interest you?

- What problems does the business have?
- Why does it have these problems?
- What solutions can you suggest?

D. Checking in. *Share your ideas with a partner. Ask your partner questions and find out about the problem. For example:*

- What is the company or business?
- What is the problem?
- What are some reasons for the problem?

Share your own opinions about the problem. Is it an interesting problem? Are there good solutions? Do you need more information?

After your discussion, add new ideas to your freewriting, if helpful.

E. *Complete the problem-solution chart for your assignment. Write the name of the company or business. Write the problems, the reasons for the problems, and possible solutions.*

Company or Business Name: _____

Problem
_____

Reasons
_____
_____
_____

Solutions
_____
_____
_____

■ THE TOPIC SENTENCE

The topic sentence of a paragraph includes the topic and controlling idea of the paragraph. In the problem-solution paragraph for this unit, the topic is the name of the company or business. The controlling idea is the problem. The topic sentence can also give background information about the topic. The background information answers questions such as:

- Where is the business?
- What is the business?

The Problem-Solution Paragraph
▼ Topic Sentence
• Topic and Controlling Idea • Background Information
▶ Body Sentences
▶ Concluding Sentence

Example:

topic   background information   controlling idea

Lucky Garden restaurant, a Chinese restaurant near my house, is always empty.

controlling idea   topic   background information

No one eats at Lucky Garden, a Chinese restaurant near my house.

Tip for Writers

Punctuation. Background information is extra information. It helps the reader understand the topic better. Use commas to separate the background information in your topic sentence. The commas show which words are part of the topic and controlling idea, and which words are part of the background information. Here are some examples.

The Royal Theater, **a movie theater in my town,** *is not popular.*

Nobody likes to see movies at The Royal Theater, **a movie theater in my town.**

Note: When the background information follows the subject, use a comma before and after the background information. When the background information is at the end of the sentence, put a comma in front of the background information.

Underline the background information. Add commas.

1. Fishermen's Bounty a local seafood store is not a good place to buy fish.

2. It is difficult to get a table at Fresh a new restaurant downtown.

3. WorldwideTransport an international delivery service is not dependable.

4. MultiStar Energy a power company hurts the environment.

5. People do not buy computers from Comp Buy a large computer company.

6. Best Shoes In Town a new shoe store in my neighborhood is not very successful.

Focused Practice

A. *Read the topic sentences. Circle the topic. Underline the controlling idea. Double underline the background information.*

Example:

(MXL Motors), an American car company, only makes luxury cars.

1. Pat's Corner, a small bookstore in my neighborhood, has very few customers.

2. Easy Auto, a local car repair shop, is not convenient.

3. A lot of young people do not like Perfect Fits, a clothing store.

4. George's Diner, the restaurant next door to our school, is usually empty.

5. No one buys computers from TechTown, a computer store downtown.

B. *Look at Exercise A. Which questions does the background information answer? Check (✓) the questions.*

	Where is the business?	**What is the business?**
1. Pat's Corner	✓	✓
2. Easy Auto		
3. Perfect Fits		
4. George's Diner		
5. TechTown		

C. *Read the paragraphs. Circle and write the best topic sentence for each paragraph. Discuss your answers with a partner.*

Paragraph 1

> ### *News for Today*
>
>
>
> The first problem is the website. Most people read news online, but the *News for Today* website is not well designed. It is difficult to read. Some sections of the newspaper are hard to find online. Another problem is that the paper does not have enough reporters to report all the local news, so people look for news on TV or in other newspapers. To solve this problem, *News for Today* should improve the website and hire more reporters. In this way, it will attract more readers.

a. *News for Today*, a local newspaper, is losing readers.

b. *News for Today* is losing readers.

c. *News for Today*, a local newspaper, has a website.

d. *News for Today* has its main office in Boston.

Paragraph 2

Problems with World Mobile

One problem is the phones. They do not work in some places. For example, I cannot use my phone in my house, so I go outside to make phone calls. Another problem is the slow data connection. For instance, it takes about 30 seconds to open a web page. Pictures or video take even longer. I think World Mobile should build more cell phone towers. It should also have a faster connection. With these solutions, service will improve and customers will be happy.

---

a. World Mobile, an international cell phone company, has many cell phones.

b. World Mobile, an international cell phone company, does not have good phone service.

c. World Mobile is not a successful company.

d. World Mobile has offices in most countries, but it does not have good phones.

D. *Read the paragraph. Work with a partner. Complete the topic sentence. Write the controlling idea.*

First Street Café

First Street Café, a restaurant near my office, _____

_____

First of all, the coffee and drinks are very expensive. For example, a cup of coffee at First Street Café costs $2.75. Most other cafés charge only $1.00. The food is expensive too. Most items on the menu are $18. That is a lot. One solution is to lower prices. First Street Café should have special prices at lunchtime. On Monday and Tuesday nights the café is not busy, so they should have special prices on those nights too. This will attract more customers and increase profits.

Your Own Writing

Planning Your Topic Sentence

A. *Look at your freewriting on page 107 and your problem-solution chart on page 108.*

Write the name of the company or business (the topic):

_____

Write a sentence about the problem (the controlling idea):

_____

Write some background information about the company or business:

_____

B. *Write your topic sentence. Use your ideas from Exercise A above.*

_____

■ THE BODY SENTENCES

The body sentences explain the controlling idea of the paragraph. They help the reader understand your topic.

In a problem-solution paragraph, the controlling idea is the problem. The body sentences explain the reasons for the problems and suggest solutions.

> **The Problem-Solution Paragraph**
>
> ▶ Topic Sentence
>
> ▼ Body Sentences
>
> • Development and Support
>   • Problems
>   • Solutions
>
> ▶ Concluding Sentence

Example:

Problems at Lucky Garden Restaurant

Lucky Garden, a Chinese restaurant near my house, is always empty. It has several problems. For one thing, the food is not fresh, and it is not good. Sometimes it is greasy or salty or very bland. Another problem is that the service is bad. The waiters are unfriendly. They are also very slow. Sometimes they bring you the wrong dish. The owners should hire a new cook and new waiters. A successful restaurant needs good food and excellent service.

The **topic** is: Lucky Garden

The **controlling idea** (the problem) is: It is always empty.

Reasons:

1. The food is not good.

2. The service is bad.

Solutions:

1. Hire a new cook.

2. Hire new waiters.

Focused Practice

A. *Read the paragraph. Answer the questions with a partner.*

Evergood Market in Trouble

Evergood Market, a small grocery store in my neighborhood, never has any customers. There are several reasons for this. The first problem is that the store looks dirty. There are empty boxes everywhere and dust on the shelves. Another problem is that the store is disorganized. Customers cannot find items easily. For example, one week the bread is at the front of the store, and the next week it is at the back. The owners should clean and reorganize the store. Then customers will feel comfortable shopping there.

---

1. What is the topic of the paragraph?

2. What is the controlling idea (the problem)?

3. What background information is there?

4. What are the reasons for the problem?

5. What are the solutions?

B. *Read the topic sentences. Check (✓) the possible reasons for the problems.*

1. **Topic Sentence:** BuyShoes.com, a big online shoe store, has poor customer service, and they do not help the customers at all.

   Reasons:

   _____ **a.** It is hard to find shoes in different sizes.

   _____ **b.** The company does not answer email.

   _____ **c.** BuyShoes.com does not sell sandals.

   _____ **d.** The customer service people are very rude.

(continued)

2. Topic Sentence: Fishermen's Bounty, a local seafood store, is not a good place to buy fish.

   Reasons:

   _____ **a.** The fish is not fresh.

   _____ **b.** The prices are too high.

   _____ **c.** Fishermen's Bounty does not sell vegetables.

   _____ **d.** Fisherman's Bounty opened last year.

3. Topic Sentence: People do not buy computers from Comp Buy, a large computer company.

   Reasons:

   _____ **a.** Comp Buy is open 24 hours a day.

   _____ **b.** Other computer stores have better prices.

   _____ **c.** Comp Buy does not sell the newest types of computers.

   _____ **d.** There are many advertisements for Comp Buy on TV.

C. *Complete the paragraph. Check (✓) and write the best solution.*

BuyShoes.com Should Change

BuyShoes.com, a big online shoe store, has poor customer service. BuyShoes.com does not help the customers at all. For example, people sometimes write email messages about problems with their orders, but the company does not answer. One time I ordered a pair of shoes, but I received the wrong color. I wrote an email, but I had to wait three weeks for an answer. Another problem is that the people are rude. They do not try to help you or apologize for their mistakes.

_____

_____

   Solutions:

   _____ **a.** BuyShoes.com should improve its website.

   _____ **b.** BuyShoes.com should hire more people to work there.

   _____ **c.** BuyShoes.com should teach its employees to be polite.

   _____ **d.** BuyShoes.com should sell fashionable shoes on its website.

D. *Work with a partner. Discuss solutions to the problem. Then write your own solution.*

Best Shoes in Town

Best Shoes In Town, a new shoe store in my neighborhood, is not very successful. It has several problems. First of all, it is hard to find shoes in many sizes, and they do not have a lot of different types of shoes. For example, they do not sell sandals. It is summertime, and a lot of people want summer shoes. Another problem is that they only have one salesperson. Service is always very slow. _____

_____

_____

Tip for Writers

Cause and Effect. When you write about a problem, you will probably write about cause and effect. What are the causes of the problem? What is the effect on the business?

Use *because* and *so* to talk about cause and effect. *Because* introduces a cause. *So* introduces an effect. A comma (,) separates the two parts of the sentence. Here are some examples.

      cause   effect
- *The music is loud,* ***so*** *you cannot hear people talk.*

        cause   effect
- ***Because*** *the music is loud, you cannot hear people talk.*

You can also use *because* in the middle of a sentence. Do not use a comma in these sentences.

      effect   cause
- *You cannot hear people talk* ***because*** *the music is loud.*

Complete the sentences. Use because *or* so.

1. _____ the service is slow, the restaurant is always empty.

2. The music is very loud, _____ you cannot hear the waiter.

3. You sometimes get the wrong dish _____ the waiters are forgetful.

4. The food is greasy, _____ it is bad for your health.

5. _____ there is only one cook, it takes a long time to get your food.

Building Word Knowledge

Descriptive Adjectives. Descriptive adjectives help the reader understand the problem and the solutions. Some descriptive adjectives are **negative**. They usually describe the **problem**. Here are some examples.

awful	greasy	rude
bland	noisy	salty
crowded	not good	unfriendly

- *The food is* **awful.** *Sometimes it is* **greasy** *or* **salty** *or very* **bland.**
- *The waiters are* **unfriendly.**

Some descriptive adjectives are **positive**. They often describe the **solutions**. Here are some examples.

comfortable	fast	good
delicious	friendly	helpful

- *The waiters should be* **friendly** *and* **helpful.**

Complete the sentences. Use the words in the box.

1.

crowded	delicious	expensive	fast	greasy	slow

Chez Henri Restaurant

You can never get a seat in this restaurant because it is always

_____. The food is _____. For example, a salad

      1.   **2.**

costs $25. You have to wait a long time for your food because the cook is

_____. The fish does not taste good because it is

      3.

_____. The solution is _____ service. A restaurant

      4.   **5.**

also needs _____ food.

            6.

2.

| comfortable | good | strong | ugly | uncomfortable | unfriendly |

Pine & Sons Furniture

The salespeople are _____. They never say "Hello" or "Thank
                              1.
you." The furniture breaks easily. It is not _____. The chairs are
                                                      2.
hard, so they are _____. The furniture does not look good. It is
                          3.
_____. The solution is _____ salespeople. They
        4.   **5.**
also need to sell _____ furniture.
                          6.

3.

| crowded | disorganized | easy | fresh | inconvenient | stale |

J&R Market

The market closes at 7 P.M. every night. The hours are _____. It is
                                                                1.
difficult to find things because it is _____. The bread stays on the
                                                2.
shelf a long time, so it is _____. The store is very small, so it is very
                                    3.
_____. One solution is to sell _____ food.
        4.   **5.**
Shopping at J&R Market should be _____ for customers.
                                          6.

Your Own Writing

Finding Out More

A. *Go online. Type the keyword* Problems *and the name of your business for the assignment. You can also type keywords such as* department store problem, grocery store problem, restaurant problem, automobile industry problem, *and* clothing industry problem. *Find information about business problems and solutions. Look at two different websites.*

B. *Write the name of the business and the websites. Write notes about the business.*

Business Name or Type of Business: _____

Website name: _____	Website name: _____
Background information: _____	Background information: _____
_____	_____
_____	_____
Problems: _____	Problems: _____
_____	_____
_____	_____
Reasons for the problems: _____	Reasons for the problems: _____
_____	_____
_____	_____
Solutions: _____	Solutions: _____
_____	_____
_____	_____

C. Checking in. *Share your information with a partner. Did your partner . . .*

- include the name of the company or business?
- write the problem?
- give background information?
- find interesting information about the problem?

After your discussion, add new ideas to your information, if helpful.

Planning Your Body Sentences

A. *Write your topic sentence from page 112. Write sentences to answer the questions below. Use your freewriting and problem-solution chart on page 108, and your notes in Finding Out More to help you.*

Topic Sentence: _____

_____

1. What problems does your business have?

_____

_____

2. Why does your business have these problems?

_____

_____

3. What are two reasons for the problems?

_____

_____

4. What are some examples?

_____

_____

5. What are some possible solutions?

_____

_____

B. Checking in. *Share your sentences with a partner. Discuss these questions.*

1. Did your partner explain the problems clearly?

2. Did your partner offer good solutions?

3. Do you have suggestions for your partner?

After your discussion, do you want to rewrite your body sentences? Make changes to the sentences, if necessary.

■ THE CONCLUDING SENTENCE

The concluding sentence is the last sentence in the paragraph. It tells the reader that the paragraph is ending. The concluding sentence often repeats or restates words or ideas from the topic sentence.

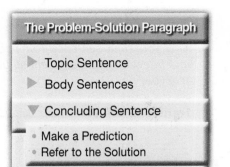

In addition, in a problem-solution paragraph, the concluding sentence can make a prediction about the solution. The prediction in your paragraph for this unit answers the questions:

- What will happen to the company?

- What will customers do?

Use *this* and *these* in the concluding sentence to refer to the solutions.

Example:

Problems at Lucky Garden Restaurant

Lucky Garden, a Chinese restaurant near my house, is always empty and for very good reasons. For one thing, the food is not fresh, and it is not good. Sometimes it is greasy or salty or very bland. Another reason is that the service is bad. The waiters are unfriendly. They are also very slow. Sometimes they bring you the wrong dish. The owners should hire a new cook and new waiters. A successful restaurant needs good food and excellent service. With these changes, Lucky Garden will have more customers and become a popular restaurant.

The **topic sentence** is: *Lucky Garden, a Chinese restaurant near my house, is always empty and for very good reasons.*

The **concluding sentence** is: *With these changes, Lucky Garden will have more customers and become a popular restaurant.*

Repeated words from the topic sentence are: *Lucky Garden; restaurant*

Restated words from the topic sentence are: *empty → have more customers / popular*

Words referring to the solutions are: *these changes → hire a new cook / hire new waiters*

The **prediction** is: *more customers and become a popular restaurant*

Focused Practice

A. *Reread the paragraph about World Mobile on page 111. Copy the concluding sentence below. Then answer the questions.*

Concluding Sentence: _____

_____

1. What prediction does the concluding sentence make?

_____

2. What does "these solutions" refer to?

_____

B. *Read the paragraph. Circle and write the concluding sentence that has a prediction and reference to the solutions.*

Pine & Sons Loses Money

    Pine & Sons, a well-known furniture store, is losing money. One problem is that people think the furniture is outdated and old-fashioned. It is an old company, so people think of the furniture in their grandparents' houses. They do not know that the company has new styles of furniture. Another problem is the price. The furniture is well made, so it is a little bit more expensive. People do not understand that it is also very high quality. It will not break or fall apart. The solution for Pine & Sons is to do more advertising. They should tell everyone that their furniture is

stylish and well made. _____

_____

---

a. In conclusion, there are several reasons why Pine & Sons is losing money.

b. Pine & Sons will be more successful some day.

c. These changes will make Pine & Sons a more popular and successful store.

C. *Read the paragraph. Write a concluding sentence and make a prediction. Compare your sentence with a partner.*

BuyShoes.com Loses Customers

BuyShoes.com, a big online shoe store, is losing customers because it has very poor customer service. The company does not help the customers at all. For example, one time I wrote an email about a problem I had. I ordered a pair of shoes, but they sent the wrong color shoes. I waited three weeks for an answer. Another problem is that the people are rude. They sent me the wrong shoes, but no one apologized for the mistake. BuyShoes.com should hire more customer service workers. They should also train the workers to be polite. _____

_____

_____

Your Own Writing

Planning Your Concluding Sentence

A. *Read your topic and body sentences from page 119. Then answer the questions.*

1. What are two or three important words from the topic sentence?

_____   _____   _____

2. What are two or three predictions about the future of the business and its customers?

_____

_____

_____

B. *Write a concluding sentence. Make a prediction about the solutions. Refer back to the solution or solutions with **this** or **these**.*

_____

_____

➡

C. Checking in. *Share your concluding sentence with a partner. Discuss these questions.*

1. Does the concluding sentence make a prediction?

2. What are some solutions to the problem? Does the concluding sentence refer to the solutions?

After your discussion, do you want to rewrite your concluding sentence? Make changes to the sentence, if necessary.

Writing Your First Draft

Write the first draft of your paragraph. Put your topic sentence, body sentences, and concluding sentence together in a paragraph. Give your paragraph a title. Hand it in to your teacher.

Step 3   Revising

Revising your work is an important part of the writing process. Revising means making your writing better by changing sentences that are not clear. Revising also means adding sentences or ideas.

Focused Practice

A. *Read the problem-solution paragraph.*

MXL Motors

MXL Motors, an American car company, lost the trust of its customers. There are several reasons customers were unsatisfied. One reason was the safety of their cars. The lights in some MXL Motors cars did not work, so there were many accidents. Customers sent 70,000 cars back to the company. The second reason is MXL Motor's response to the problems. The company did not report the problems for several months, so customers were unhappy and confused. To solve this problem, MXL Motors should fix the safety problems. They should pay for the repairs to the cars. They should also explain the problems to their customers. This will increase trust and make MXL Motors popular again.

B. *Work with a partner. Answer the questions about the paragraph.*

1. What is the topic of the paragraph? Circle it.

2. What it is the controlling idea (the problem)? Underline it.

3. What is the background information about the company? Underline it two times.

4. What are the reasons for the problem? Put a star (*) next to the two reasons.

(continued)

5. What are the solutions? Put a plus (+) next to the solutions.

6. Is there a concluding sentence? Underline it. Does it make a prediction for the future?

Your Own Writing

Revising Your Draft

A. *Reread the first draft of your paragraph. Use the Revision Checklist. What do you need to revise?*

B. *Revise your paragraph.*

Revision Checklist
Did you . . .
☐ describe a business problem?
☐ state the problem in the topic sentence?
☐ give background information about the business?
☐ explain the reasons for the problem?
☐ suggest a solution?
☐ make a prediction in the concluding sentence?
☐ write about cause and effect?

Step 4   Editing

■ GRAMMAR PRESENTATION

Before you hand in your revised paragraph, read it again and look for errors in spelling, capitalization, punctuation, and grammar. In this section, you will review count and non-count nouns. Think about your paragraph as you review.

Count and Non-Count Nouns

Grammar Notes	Examples
1. Count nouns refer to separate things. It is easy to count them.	• one **store**, two **stores**, three **stores**
To form the plural of most count nouns, add **-s** or **-es**	• problem problem**s** • business business**es**
Some plural count nouns are irregular. Do not add -s to make the plural form.	• child children

2. Non-count nouns refer to things that are difficult to count.

Abstract ideas (*safety, customer service*) and **food and drinks** (*pizza, coffee*) are often non-count.

- That store needs more **advertising**.
- The customers worry about **safety**.
- First Street Café sells **coffee**.

3. Use **singular verbs** with **non-count nouns**.

- Safety **is** important.
- Advertising **is** one solution.

4. Use *a* or *an* before **singular count nouns**. Use *a* before words that start with consonant sounds. Use *an* before words that start with vowel sounds.

- MXL Motors is **a c**ar company.
- There is **a p**roblem.
- I have **an i**dea.
- It lasted **an h**our.

Use *some* (or nothing) with **plural count nouns** and **non-count nouns**.

- They can hire (some) **more waiters**.
- They need (some) **new advertising**.

Focused Practice

A. *Read the sentences. Circle the non-count nouns. Underline the count nouns.*

1. Customers did not like the pizza.

2. The company has excellent customer service.

3. Advertising helps businesses.

4. Shoppers want to buy good clothing.

5. Safety is important to most customers.

6. The store is having a sale.

7. Honesty is very important.

8. Every problem has a solution.

9. The restaurant has many problems.

10. Some waiters at the restaurant were rude.

B. *Complete the sentences. Use* a, an, *or* some.

1. Domino's is _____ pizza maker.

2. Some people do not want to buy _____ car from MXL Motors.

3. Lucky Garden should offer _____ fresh fish.

4. You can find _____ information about BuyShoes.com online.

5. Here is _____ idea. It can help solve Evergood Market's problem.

6. I waited _____ hour for my food.

7. It is _____ hard problem to solve.

8. SuperNet is attracting _____ customers.

C. *Read the paragraph. Correct six more count or non-count errors.*

What Is Wrong with Perfect Fits?

Young people do not like to shop at Perfect Fits, a clothing store in downtown
Houston. One problem is that the ~~clothings~~ *clothing* is expensive. For example, a shirts costs
$80. The second problem is the customer service are not good. You have to wait a
long time for a employee to help you. I think the solution is to hire more workers
and have many sale. These change will attract a young people to Perfect Fits.

D. *Write five sentences for your assignment. Use count and non-count nouns. They can be sentences
you already have in your paragraph, or they can be new sentences.*

1. _____

2. _____

3. _____

4. _____

5. _____

Your Own Writing

Editing Your Draft

A. *Edit your paragraph for the assignment. Use the Editing Checklist below.*

B. *Write a clean copy of your paragraph.*

Editing Checklist

Did you . . .

☐ use count and non-count nouns correctly?

☐ use new vocabulary from the unit?

☐ use *so* and *because* for cause and effect?

☐ use *this* and *these* and refer to solutions?

☐ format the paragraph correctly?

☐ give your paragraph a title?

☐ use correct capitalization and punctuation?

6 Alone or Together?

IN THIS UNIT You will write a compare-contrast paragraph about activities you do with people and activities you do by yourself.

There are many activities that you can do alone, or with a group of people. When you are alone, you can do the things you want to do. You do not have to worry about other people. When you are in a group, you can enjoy the company of other people. You have people to talk to or help you. What activities do you enjoy doing alone? What do you enjoy doing in a group?

Planning for Writing

■BRAINSTORM

A. *Read the paragraph. When do you feel solitude? When do you feel loneliness? Discuss the questions with a partner.*

Solitude or Loneliness

Solitude and *loneliness* are similar words. Both words describe feeling *alone*, but the words have very different meanings. People enjoy solitude. They are away from other people, but they feel happy. Many activities can give you a feeling of solitude: taking a walk alone on the beach, listening to music with headphones, or just spending time by yourself. In contrast, loneliness is a kind of sadness. People feel unhappy because they are alone. People often feel lonely when they are in a new place and do not know anyone, or when they are away from the people they love. Next time you feel alone, ask yourself: Is the feeling *solitude* or *loneliness*?

B. Using a Venn Diagram. A Venn diagram helps you think about the similarities and differences between two things. It answers the questions: How are two things similar? How are they different?

Read the paragraph in Exercise A again. Work with a partner. Write the words in the Venn diagram.

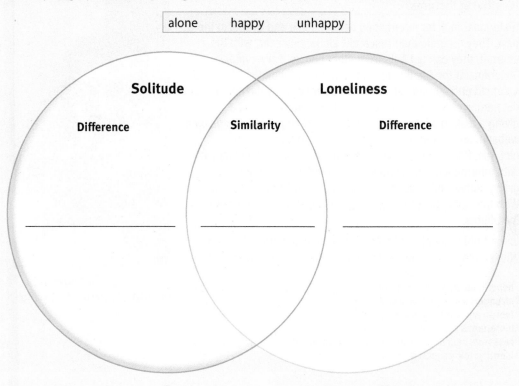

alone   happy   unhappy

Solitude   Loneliness

Difference   Similarity   Difference

Read the Web article about new types of group activities.

Together Is Better Than Alone

1. Many people choose to do activities together rather than alone. For example, group tours are popular with travelers. In school, students often study in groups. Group activities have many benefits:[1] People can share the costs, share the work, and have more fun. For this reason, people are always finding new ways to do things in groups.

Group Weddings

2. Group weddings are becoming popular. A wedding ceremony usually has one couple, but in a group wedding, many couples get married at the same time, in the same place. A group wedding may sound strange, but it has many benefits. Couples can share the cost of a big and beautiful space, the food, transportation, and entertainment. There are also a lot of people to celebrate when the ceremony is over. Group weddings are not only more popular these days, they are getting bigger too. For example, over 2,000 couples married in a recent group wedding in Xiamen, China.

Sharing the Cost of a Car

3. Most cars belong to one person or family, but cars are expensive so many people choose to share the cost of a car. Today, there are businesses designed to help strangers[2] share the cost of a car. People pay a monthly fee[3] to share cars with other customers. The company pays for the car, gas, insurance, parking, and other costs. Jarrod Shmall, 27, often uses a shared car near his house in London. "I only need a car once or twice a week," he says, "so I don't need a car by myself."

Identifying Pictures

4. Historians[4] look for information about people and events in the past. They often do their research[5] alone. However, with the Internet, they can get help from other people. For example, historians at the Smithsonian Museum in Washington, D.C., had a lot of old photographs of women in science. They did not know the names of the women, so they tried *crowdsourcing*, a way of giving a task to a large group of people. They put the photos on a website, and asked people to identify[6] the women in the pictures. People saw the photos and wrote to the Smithsonian with information. One woman saw a photograph of her grandmother and gave the Smithsonian details about her career. With this help, the Smithsonian identified many of the women in the photos.

5. In the future, people will find other activities to try in a group. With so many benefits, group work makes a lot of sense.

Elizabeth Sabin Goodwin, identified by crowdsourcing

---

[1] **benefit:** an advantage, improvement, or help that you get from something
[2] **stranger:** someone that you do not know
[3] **fee:** an amount of money you pay
[4] **historian:** a person who studies history
[5] **research:** serious study of a subject to discover new facts about it
[6] **identify:** to recognize someone

Building Word Knowledge

Compound Nouns. Two nouns often go together to make compound nouns. In a compound noun, the first noun describes the following noun. Sometimes they are one word, as in *teamwork*. Other times they are two words, as in *group wedding* and *group activities*. Sometimes a dictionary can help you find and spell compound nouns. Learn common compound nouns to increase your vocabulary. Here are some examples.

Noun + Noun	=	Compound Noun
team	*work*	*teamwork:* working together in a team
team	*mate*	*teammate:* a person who works on a team
team	*sport*	*a team sport:* a sport people play in teams, such as soccer
group	*wedding*	*a group wedding:* a wedding people have as a group
group	*travel*	*group travel:* travel people do together as a group

Circle the compound noun in each sentence.

1. Group weddings are easy, fun, and cheap.

2. Teamwork is important in business.

3. The class is doing a group project.

4. My teammates worked together to win the game.

5. I like group activities because we can share information and learn from each other.

6. I prefer individual sports. I am not very good at team sports.

Focused Practice

A. *Read the Web article on page 130 again. Complete the sentences. Circle the correct word.*

1. The reading is mainly about _____.

    a. individual activities

    b. group activities

    c. new experiences

2. The reading gives examples of activities. People usually do these activities _____.

    a. in groups

    b. in families

    c. by themselves

3. According to the author, group activities can _____.

    a. take more time

    b. be more difficult

    c. save time and money

B. *Read the sentences. Are the sentences True (T) or False (F)? Write T or F.*

T **1.** Group weddings are less expensive than individual weddings.

T **2.** Most weddings in China are group weddings.

T **3.** With car-sharing companies, customers share cars with people they do not know.

F **4.** Jarrod Shmall always drives to work.

F **5.** The Smithsonian had photographs of women scientists who are still alive.

F **6.** One historian at the Smithsonian identified all the photographs of women scientists.

C. *Discuss your answers with a small group.*

1. Would you like to join a group wedding? Try car sharing? Help do research through crowdsourcing? Why or why not?

2. The article described the advantages of group activities. What are some disadvantages?

3. What are other individual activities that people sometimes do in groups?

Writing a Compare-Contrast Paragraph

In this unit, you are going to write a compare-contrast paragraph. A compare-contrast paragraph explains the similarities (comparisons) and differences (contrasts) between two things. It uses examples to give the reader a clear picture about the similarities and differences. A compare-contrast paragraph is like other paragraphs: It has a topic sentence with a controlling idea, body sentences that support the controlling idea, and a concluding sentence.

> **The Compare-Contrast Paragraph**
>
> ▶ Topic Sentence
> ▶ Body Sentences
> ▶ Concluding Sentence

Step 1   Prewriting

Prewriting is an important step in the writing process. It helps you choose your topic and get ideas for your paragraph. In this prewriting, first you choose your assignment. Then you use a Venn diagram to get ideas for your paragraph.

Your Own Writing

Choosing Your Assignment

A. *Choose Assignment 1 or Assignment 2.*

Assignment 1: Write about an activity you do at school or work. Compare and contrast the activity when you do it alone and when you do it in a group.

Assignment 2: Write about an activity you do for fun. Compare and contrast the activity when you do it alone and when you do it in a group.

B. *Make a list of activities. Use the ideas below or your own ideas. Check (✔) the activities you like to do alone and the activities you like to do in a group. Then choose an activity for your assignment.*

Activities at School or Work	Alone	In a Group
Write a report	✓	
Study for a test	✓	
Give a presentation	✓	
Your own ideas:		

Activities for Fun	Alone	In a Group
Play soccer		
Eat at a restaurant		✓
Watch TV		✓
Your own ideas:		
group travel		✓

Alone or Together?   **133**

C. *Freewrite for five minutes about the activity for your assignment. Write any ideas you have about the topic. Here are some questions to get you started.*

- What is the activity?
- What do you enjoy about the activity?
- When do you do this activity? Do you do it at work, at school, or for fun?
- Do you prefer to do this activity with friends, or by yourself?
- Why do you do it in a group? What do you like about it?
- Why do you do it alone? What do you like about it?

D. Checking in. *Share your ideas with a partner. Ask your partner questions about the activities.*

For example:

- What activities do you like to do alone? Why?
- What activities do you like to do in a group? Why?
- Where do you do these activities?

After your discussion, add new ideas to your freewriting, if helpful.

E. *Complete the Venn diagram for your assignment. Write the name of the activity. Write the differences between doing the activity alone and in a group. Write the similarities.*

Activity: _____

Alone   **In a Group**

Differences   **Similarities**   **Differences**

_____   _____   _____

_____   _____   _____

_____   _____   _____

_____   _____   _____

Step 2 Writing the First Draft

■ THE TOPIC SENTENCE

The topic sentence gets the reader ready to read the paragraph. It includes the topic and controlling idea of the paragraph. In the topic sentence of a compare-contrast paragraph, the topic is the two ideas you are comparing. The controlling idea is the type of comparison. When you compare two things, you describe their similarities. When you contrast two things, you describe their differences.

The Compare-Contrast Paragraph
▼ Topic Sentence
• Topic and Controlling Idea • Compare and Contrast
▶ Body Sentences
▶ Concluding Sentence

Example:

There are similarities and differences between working at home alone and working at an office with other people.

The **topic** is: Working at home alone and working in an office with other people.

The **controlling idea** is: There are similarities and differences.

Building Word Knowledge

Activities. Many verbs describe activities. Often the name of the activity (the noun) is the gerund form of the verb, that is, the verb + -*ing*. To increase your vocabulary, learn the gerund form of activity verbs when you learn the verbs. A dictionary can help you spell these words. Here are some examples.

Verb	Noun	
bicycle	bicycling	*I **bicycle** every day with friends. **Bicycling** is good exercise.*
travel	traveling	*My friends and I **travel** every summer. **Traveling** with friends is more fun than **traveling** alone.*
listen	listening	*I **listen** to music a lot. **Listening** to music relaxes me*

Complete the sentences. Use the gerund form of the verbs. Use a dictionary to help you with spelling.

1. I usually **study** by myself. _____ alone is better than

   _____ in a group.

2. On weekends, my friends and I **watch** movies at my house. _____

   movies with friends is more enjoyable than _____ movies alone.

3. I help my mother and father **cook** dinner. _____ dinner with my

   family is fun.

4. I **live** by myself. _____ alone is better for me than

   _____ with a roommate.

(continued)

Alone or Together? **135**

5. I **drive** to work in a carpool with two other people. _driving_ in a carpool

is more relaxing than _driving_ alone.

Focused Practice

A. *Read the topic sentences. Circle the topic (the two activities). Underline the controlling idea (the comparison).*

Example:

There are some similarities and differences between group weddings and traditional weddings.

1. There are some similarities and differences between traveling alone and traveling in a group.

2. Individual sports and team sports have similarities and differences.

3. Eating in a restaurant alone and eating with a group are similar, but there are some important differences.

B. *Read the paragraphs. Circle and write the best topic sentence for each paragraph. Make sure that the topic sentence compares two activities.*

Paragraph 1

Carpooling to Work

_____

_____

I carpool to work with two other people. Each day, a different person drives. The distance to work is the same, and we use the same amount of gas. However, driving in a carpool is less expensive. I do not have to drive my car five days a week. Instead, I only drive one or two days a week, so I spend less money on gas. Another difference is the amount of pollution. We drive one car a day, not three cars. This makes less pollution and is better for the environment.

---

a. I drive to work in a carpool because it saves money and reduces pollution.

b. Driving to work alone is expensive and bad for the environment.

c. Driving to work in a carpool and driving alone are similar, but there are some important differences.

d. Some people drive to work in a carpool, and others drive to work alone.

Paragraph 2

Traveling

_____

_____

Both types of travel are fun and interesting, but one difference is the amount of freedom you have. Traveling alone gives you more freedom. You can do whatever you want. In a group, everyone has to agree to a plan. However, traveling alone is more expensive. You cannot share the cost of a room or a meal. You have to pay for everything by yourself.

---

a. Traveling with a group is better than traveling alone.

b. There are similarities and differences between traveling alone and traveling with a group.

c. Traveling alone is more dangerous than traveling with a group.

e. Traveling alone and traveling in a group are both fun ways to travel.

C. *Read the paragraph. Work with a partner. Write the two activities in the paragraph. Then write a topic sentence that compares the two activities.*

Skiing Made Fun

_____

_____

I really like both types of skiing. They are both good exercise and great fun on vacation. However, one difference is that skiing alone is more exciting than skiing in a group. When I ski alone, I go on the most difficult mountains. I do not have to worry about others. However, skiing alone can be dangerous. If I fall and get hurt, no one can help me. So I always think carefully before skiing alone or with friends.

Activity 1: Skiing alone in a group both have advanges

Activity 2: _____

HW ✓

Your Own Writing

Planning Your Topic Sentence

A. *Look at your freewriting and your Venn diagram on page 134. Write the name of the activities you will compare.*

_____dancing_____ alone

_____dancing_____ in a group

B. *Write a topic sentence comparing the two activities above. Complete each sentence with the activities. Then choose one sentence for your assignment.*

1. There are some similarities and differences between _dancing alone_

   and _dancing in a group._

2. _dancing alone_ and _dancing in group_ have similarities

   and differences.

3. _dancing alone_ and _dancing in group_ are similar, but

   there are some important differences.

C. Checking in. *Share your sentences with a partner. Discuss these questions.*

   • Is the topic clear?

   • Does the topic sentence compare an activity you do by yourself and in a group?

   After your discussion, do you want to rewrite your body sentences? Make changes to the sentences, if necessary.

■ THE BODY SENTENCES

The body sentences of a paragraph explain the topic sentence. They give details and examples to make the controlling idea clear. In a compare-contrast paragraph, the topic sentence makes a comparison. The body sentences explain the comparison. They answer the question: How are two things similar and different?

Include details and examples to explain the differences to the reader. Describe the things that make the two activities different.

The Compare-Contrast Paragraph
▶ Topic Sentence
▼ Body Sentences
• Organization • Similarities and Differences
▶ Concluding Sentence

I like dancing alone for my relex and for exerciase.
   but dancing in group can be fun, because you have more opportunity for differents ways the dancing, for instance Tango and Salsa dances.

Organization

There are several ways to organize the ideas in a compare-contrast paragraph. One way to organize the ideas is:

- first describe the similarities
- then describe the differences

This organization helps your reader understand the comparisons and contrasts in the paragraph.

Example:

The Best Way to Work

There are similarities and differences between working at home alone and working at an office with other people. On most days, I work in a big office, but on Friday I work at home. At both places, I do the same work. I also work with the same people. However, there are some important differences. My office is more distracting. People always stop at my desk to talk. I can also hear my coworkers' phone conversations. In contrast, my home is quieter. No one bothers me, and I can focus on my work. For these reasons, I like to work at home.

The **topic** is: *working at home and working in an office with other people*

The **controlling idea** is: *There are similarities and differences*

The **similarities** are: *I do the same work. I also work with the same people.*

The **differences** are: *My office is more distracting. My home is quieter.*

The **details and examples** for *My office is more distracting* are: *People stop by desk to talk. I can hear my coworkers' phone conversations.*

The **details and examples** for *My home is quieter* are: *No one bothers me. I can focus on my work.*

the most interesting similiarities and differences between dancing alone and in grup are

Building Word Knowledge

Words for Similarity and Difference. The following words will be helpful to you when you write your compare-contrast paragraph.

Words for Similarity	Words for Difference
both	in contrast
similar	but
the same	however
also	another difference
	different

A. *Read the paragraph "The Best Way to Work" on page 139 again. Underline the words for similarity and difference.*

B. *Complete the paragraph. Use the words in the box.*

another difference	both	different	however	the same

Playing the Violin

People think that playing solo violin and playing violin in an orchestra are the same, but there are important differences. One similarity is the performance. In ___both___ types of performances, you play onstage before hundreds of people. The preparation is also ___the same___. You practice for hours a day. However, the stress level is ___different___. Playing solo is more stressful. Everyone can hear your mistakes. In contrast, playing in an orchestra is often more relaxing. You can follow the other musicians. The audience usually does not notice your mistakes. ___Onethe diff___ is the type of music. When you play solo, you can play any piece of music, in any style you like. ___however___, when you play in an orchestra, you have less freedom. You have to play like everyone else. That is why I like to play solo violin.

Focused Practice

A. *Read the paragraph. Answer the questions with a partner.*

> **Jogging**
>
> *TS cooper*
>
> Jogging alone and jogging with a friend are similar, but there are some important differences. Jogging is a good way to stay healthy, and you can do it anywhere. However, jogging with a friend is better. For example, sometimes I jog with my friend Carl. When I'm alone, I get tired easily and want to stop. In contrast, Carl encourages me. He says, "Keep going, you can do it!" This helps me continue. Jogging with Carl is also more fun. I get bored jogging by myself, but Carl and I talk to each other when we jog. We tell jokes and interesting stories. It makes the time go by quickly.

1. What is the topic of the paragraph? Circle the two activities.
2. What is the controlling idea (the comparison)? Underline it.
3. What are the similarities? Put a check (✓) next to them. *good way to stay healthy. do it anywhere.*
4. What are the differences? Put a star (*) next to them.
5. What details and examples explain the differences? Underline them two times.

4 alone: get tired easily. you get bored.

5 In Contrast. carl. encourages He. Keep g... Help he continue the time go quickly.

HW

B. *Read the paragraphs. Complete the paragraphs with the information in the box.*

Paragraph 1

1. eating alone is more relaxing
2. I enjoy the same great food and service at the restaurant when I am alone or with friends
3. eating alone is usually more expensive

Eating at a Restaurant: Alone or Not Alone

Eating at a restaurant alone and eating in a restaurant with a group of friends

are similar. I *enjoy the same great food and service*
at the restaurant when I'm alone or with friends.

However, there are some important differences. For example, *eating alone*
is usually more expensive.

I do not have to talk. I can sit quietly, enjoy the food, and think about my day.

Another difference is that *eating alone is more*
relaxing.

My friends and I share the dishes and divide the check. When I'm alone, I have to

pay for everything myself.

142 UNIT 6

Paragraph 2

1   2   3

the feeling of teamwork	group projects are easier	help you learn

Two Ways to Do Research Projects

There are similarities and differences between group research projects and individual research projects. Both types of projects _____ 3 _____

_____. They make you read a lot and explain the information in a new way. However, _____ 1 _____

_____. For example, you do not have to do all the research by yourself. You can share the work with other students. Another difference is _____ 2 _____

_____.

Working on a project in groups creates teamwork. You get to know your classmates well and feel a strong connection to them.

HW

Paragraph 3

1
2
3
| are cheaper than eating at a restaurant |
| you can learn from the other person |
| cooking with another person is much faster |

Cooking Alone: The Pros and Cons

There are similarities and differences between cooking alone and cooking with another person. Both types of cooking __1_____

_____.

They are both a lot of fun. However, there are some differences. For example,

_____,

_____3_____.

One person can cut the food, another can work at the stove, and cooking takes less time. In contrast, when you cook alone you do everything yourself. Another difference is that _____2_____

_____.

I often cook with my brother. He is a great cook, and he teaches me new recipes.

C. *Read the paragraphs in Exercise B again. Circle the words for similarities and differences in each paragraph. Compare your answers with a partner.*

Your Own Writing

Finding Out More

A. *Go online. Type the name of the activity that you are writing about, such as* **cooking** *or* **bicycling.** *Look for new ideas and new words for your compare-contrast paragraph. Look at two different websites.*

B. *Write the name of the activity. Try to answer the questions about information on each website.*

Name of the Activity: _____

1. Who does the activity? Write the names of the people.

Website 1: _____

Website 2: _____

2. Where do the people do the activity? Write the places.

Website 1: _____

Website 2: _____

3. When do people do the activity? Write the dates, days, seasons, or time.

Website 1: _____

Website 2: _____

4. What equipment do people need to do the activity? List the equipment, such as a bicycle, a computer, a cookbook, or a car.

Website 1: _____

Website 2: _____

5. Why do people do the activity? List words, such as *fun, healthy,* or *class assignment.*

Website 1: _____

Website 2: _____

C. Checking in. *Share your information with a partner. Did your partner find . . .*

- information to answer the questions in the chart?
- interesting information about the activity?

After your discussion, add new ideas to your notes, if helpful.

Planning Your Body Sentences

A. *Write your topic sentence from page 138. Write two similarities and two differences. Write examples and details to support them. Use your Venn diagram and your freewriting on page 134, and your notes from the websites to help you.*

Topic Sentence: _____

Similarity (comparison) 1: _____

Examples: _____

_____

Similarity 2: _____

Examples: _____

_____

Difference (contrast) 1: _____

Examples: _____

_____

Difference 2: _____

Examples: _____

_____

B. Checking in. *Share your sentences with a partner. Discuss these questions.*

1. What are the similarities and differences? Are they clear?

2. Do the examples help explain the similarities and differences?

3. Are there any details that do not support the controlling idea?

4. Which details are the most interesting?

5. Does your partner need to add more information to make anything clearer? What can your partner add?

After your discussion, do you want to rewrite your body sentences? Make changes, if necessary.

■THE CONCLUDING SENTENCE

The concluding sentence ends the paragraph, but there are many different ways to write the concluding sentence. In this book, you learned to:

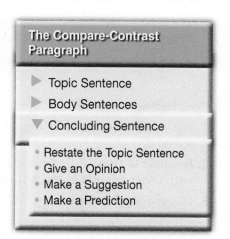

- repeat and restate the topic sentence in a different way (see Units 1 and 2)

- add a final thought or comment about the experience (see Unit 3)

- give advice to the reader (see Unit 4)

- make a prediction about the future (see Unit 5)

You can end a compare-contrast paragraph in any of these ways. Choose the way that explains your ideas and works best for your paragraph.

Remember: You can introduce your concluding sentence with transition words. In this book, you learned these transitions:

- *for these reasons, clearly* (see Unit 4)

- *this, these* (see Unit 5)

Example:

The Best Way to Work

There are similarities and differences between working at home alone and working in an office with other people. On most days, I work in a big office, but on Friday I work at home. At both places, I do the same work. I also work with the same people. However, there are some important differences. My office is more distracting. People always stop at my desk to talk. I can also hear my coworkers' phone conversations. In contrast, my home is quieter. No one bothers me, and I can focus on my work. _____

Possible concluding sentences:

Repeat and restate the controlling idea:

- *As you can see, there are important differences between working at home and working at an office.*

Add a final thought:

- *Because of these differences, I prefer to work at home.*

Give advice:

- *Clearly, everyone should work at home part of the time.*

Make a prediction:

- *For these reasons, I will try to work at home more in the future.*

Focused Practice

A. *Read the topic sentence from the paragraph* Jogging *on page 141. Then read the concluding sentences below. Match each sentence with the type of concluding sentence.*

Topic Sentence: There are similarities and differences between jogging alone and jogging with a friend.

Concluding Sentence

1. For these reasons, I like to go jogging with a friend.

2. Because of these differences, I plan to jog with other friends in the future.

3. Clearly, jogging with a friend and jogging alone are very different.

4. People should jog together so they can have fun.

Type

_____ **a.** Restate the controlling idea.

_____ **b.** Add a final thought.

_____ **c.** Give advice.

_____ **d.** Make a prediction.

B. *Read the paragraph. Work with a partner. Write four concluding sentences for the paragraph.*

Cleaning—With a Group or Alone?

There are similarities and differences between cleaning your house alone and cleaning with other people. The amount of work is the same. However, cleaning with other people is easier because you can share the work. For example, my family always cleans house together. Each person cleans a different room in the house. We finish very quickly. Cleaning with others is more fun too. When my family and I clean the house, we put on loud music. We dance around and sing. It makes the work go quickly. _____

---

1. Restate the controlling idea.

_____

_____

2. Add a final thought.

_____

_____

3. Give advice.

_____

_____

4. Make a prediction.

_____

_____

C. *Choose your favorite concluding sentence. Share it with the class.*

Your Own Writing

Planning Your Concluding Sentence

A. *Write your topic sentence from page 146. Then write four concluding sentences.*

Topic Sentence: _____

1. Restate the controlling idea.

_____

_____

2. Add a final thought.

_____

_____

3. Give advice.

_____

_____

4. Make a prediction.

_____

_____

B. Checking in. *Share your concluding sentence with a partner. Discuss these questions.*

1. Which concluding sentence is best for the paragraph? Why?

2. Do you need to change the concluding sentence to make it better? How?

After your discussion, do you want to rewrite your concluding sentences? Make changes to the sentences, if necessary.

C. *Write the concluding sentence for your paragraph.*

Concluding Sentence: _____

_____

Writing Your First Draft

Write the first draft of your paragraph. Put your topic sentence, body sentences, and concluding sentence together in a paragraph. Give your paragraph a title. Hand in your first draft to your teacher.

Step 3   Revising

Revising your work is an important part of the writing process. Revising means you can change your writing. You can make your writing clearer, more correct, and more interesting. One way to make your paragraph more interesting is to use different types of sentences. You may want to revise your sentences and add variety.

Tip for Writers

Sentence Variety. Good writers use different types of sentences in their writing. In this book, you learned about three types of sentences: simple sentences, compound sentences, and complex sentences. Use all three types of sentences in your writing. This way, your writing is more interesting to read.

A **simple sentence** has a subject and verb. It expresses a complete idea.
I play piano.
Teamwork is important.

A **compound sentence** connects two ideas using *and, but, or,* and *so*.
*I cook dinner, **and** my roommate washes dishes.*
*A normal wedding is expensive, **but** a group wedding is cheap.*

A **complex sentence** connects two ideas using *because*.
*I share a car **because** it is cheaper.*

Read the sentences. Are they simple sentences (S), compound sentences (CO), or complex sentences (CX)? Write S, CO, *or* CX.

_____ **1.** Skiing alone is dangerous, but skiing with friends is usually safe.

_____ **2.** Because I am a student, I need to do group work.

_____ **3.** Some people prefer individual sports.

_____ **4.** I work from home, so I usually eat lunch by myself.

_____ **5.** I exercise with a friend because it is more fun.

Focused Practice

A. *Read the compare-contrast paragraph.*

Giving Presentations

Giving a group presentation is similar to giving an individual presentation, but there are some important differences. You need to do research and practice for both presentations. You also have to organize the information for your presentation. However, a group presentation is harder than an individual presentation because you have to work well with everyone in the group. You also have to meet outside of class and plan the presentation. The other difference is the grade. In an individual presentation, you get a grade for your work only. In a group presentation, you get a grade for the work by people in the group. For these reasons, I like giving individual presentations.

B. *Work with a partner. Answer the questions about the paragraph.*

1. What is the topic of the paragraph? Circle the two activities.
2. What similarities does the writer describe? Check (✓) them.
3. What differences does the writer describe? Put a star (*) next to them.
4. What details or examples of the differences does the writer give? Underline them.
5. Is there a concluding sentence? Underline it two times.
6. What type of concluding sentence does the writer have? _____

   _____

7. Is there sentence variety? What types of sentences are there?
   Check (✓) the types.

   ❑ simple sentences

   ❑ compound sentences

   ❑ complex sentences

Your Own Writing

Revising Your Draft

A. *Reread the first draft of your paragraph. Use the Revision Checklist. What do you need to revise?*

B. *Revise your paragraph.*

Revision Checklist
Did you . . .
☐ compare and contrast an activity you do by yourself and in a group?
☐ include a topic sentence with a controlling idea?
☐ include similarities and differences in the body sentences?
☐ give examples and details of the similarities and differences?
☐ include a concluding sentence?
☐ use a variety of sentence types?
☐ use new vocabulary words from this unit?

■ GRAMMAR PRESENTATION

Before you hand in your revised paragraph, read it again and look for errors in grammar, punctuation, and spelling. In this section, you will review comparative adjectives. Think about your paragraph as you review.

Comparative Adjectives

Grammar Notes	Examples
1. Use the **comparative form of an adjective + *than*** to compare two activities, people, or things.	• Group weddings are **cheaper than** traditional weddings. • Cleaning in groups is **faster than** cleaning alone.
2. To form the comparative of **short (one-syllable) adjectives**, add **-er** to the adjective. If the adjective ends in -e, add only -r.	• Singing alone is **harder** than singing with a friend. • Driving alone is **safer** than driving with others.
3. To form the comparative of adjectives that end in **a consonant + y**, change the **y** to **i** and add **-er**. *busy - **busier*** *easy - **easier*** *heavy - **heavier***	• Working together is **easier than** working alone.
4. To form the comparative of most adjectives of **two or more syllables**, use ***more*** before the adjective. *expensive - **more expensive*** *intelligent - **more intelligent*** **BE CAREFUL!** Do not use two comparative forms together.	• Driving at night is **more dangerous**. • Traditional weddings are **more expensive than** group weddings. • Working together is **easier**. NOT: Working together is ~~more~~ easier.
5. The adjectives ***good*** and ***bad*** have irregular comparative forms. *good - **better*** *bad - **worse***	• Working at home is **better than** working in an office. • Loneliness feels **worse than** solitude.

Focused Practice

A. *Read the brochure. Complete the sentences. Write the correct comparative adjective.*

MOUNT VISTA TOUR COMPANY

Join us for a tour of beautiful Mount Vista! Choose your tour option below.

	Group Tour	Private Tour
Price	$11.00 per person	$24.00 per person
Length of tour	1 hour	2 hours
Difficulty	Easy – walk on the road	Difficult – climb the mountain
Times	10:00 A.M. Monday – Friday	6:00 A.M. Monday – Friday
Reviews	** You can't see much. I didn't get many good pictures.	**** Great views! I took a lot of beautiful pictures.

1. The group tour is _____ than the private tour.
   (cheaper / more expensive)

2. The group tour is _____ than the private tour.
   (longer / shorter)

3. The group tour is _____ than the private tour.
   (harder / easier)

4. The private tour is _____ in the day.
   (earlier / later)

5. The view on the group tour is _____.
   (better / worse)

B. *Complete the sentences with comparative adjectives. Use your own ideas.*

1. Traveling alone is _____ traveling in a group.

2. Studying in a group is _____ studying by yourself.

3. Living by yourself is _____ living with others.

4. Team sports are _____ individual sports.

5. Cleaning your house by yourself is _____ cleaning in a group.

6. Working at home is _____ working in an office.

7. Eating alone is _____ eating with others.

8. Walking on the beach with a friend is _____ walking on the beach by yourself.

C. *Read the paragraph. Correct seven more comparative adjective errors.*

Living Alone Or with Roommates

        better

You can live alone or with a roommate, but which is ~~more better~~? Living with a roommate is more noisy. For example, my roommate always stays awake late than I do. He sometimes watches TV when I am trying to sleep. However, living with a roommate is more cheaper. Cleaning is easyer too. We can finish more fast. Another difference is that living with others is enjoyable than living alone. I always have someone to talk to at home. Overall, I think living with a roommate is gooder than living alone.

D. *Write five sentences for your assignment. Use comparative adjectives. The sentences can be ones you already have in your paragraph, or they can be new sentences.*

1. _____

2. _____

3. _____

4. _____

5. _____

Your Own Writing

Editing Your Draft

A. *Edit your paragraph for the assignment. Use the Editing Checklist below.*

B. *Write a clean copy of your paragraph. Give it to your teacher.*

Editing Checklist

Did you . . .

☐ use comparative adjectives correctly?

☐ use transition words correctly?

☐ choose an appropriate type of concluding sentence to explain your ideas?

☐ format the paragraph correctly?

☐ give your paragraph a title?

☐ check spelling, punctuation, and capitalization?

Index

Acknowledgments

The authors would like to thank Penny Laporte and Debbie Sistino for their assistance and feedback during development of this book. We would also like to thank our families for their patience and support during the writing process.

Credits

survery = Pesquisa.

- newsineasyenglish.com
- use name: renata costa santos
- beatriz 69
- give up: desistir / entregar / deliver / eeder
-

IF you never TRY, you'll never know!